Robert Browning
and
Julia Wedgwood

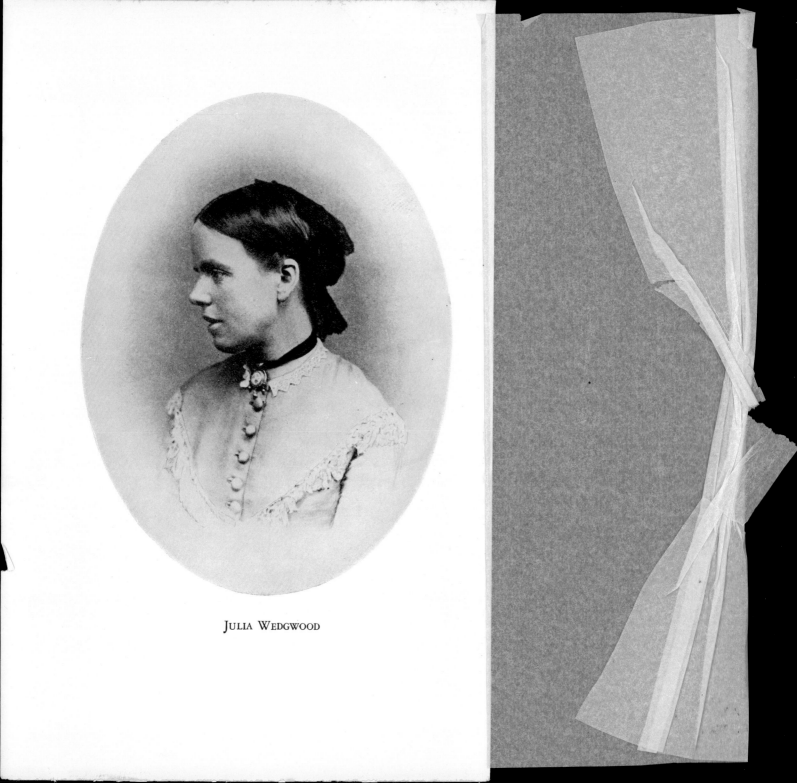

JULIA WEDGWOOD

Robert Browning

and

Julia Wedgwood

A Broken Friendship as Revealed by

Their Letters

Edited by Richard Curle

FREDERICK A. STOKES COMPANY
NEW YORK   MCMXXXVII

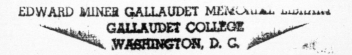

Printed in the United States of America

ILLUSTRATIONS

INTRODUCTION

THIS remarkable correspondence between Robert Browning and Julia Wedgwood came to light through the death, in 1935, of Miss Wedgwood's younger sister at the age of ninety-one. This lady, who had married her cousin, was Mrs. Godfrey Wedgwood of Staffordshire; and it was her daughter, and only child, who some time after her mother's death handed me the Browning half of the correspondence to look through, with the idea that it might contain matters of interest. It was not till the middle of 1936 that Julia Wedgwood's own letters were found. They had evidently been returned to her after Browning died: like his letters they had been done up in a bundle and put away in a drawer.

The very existence of such a correspondence has been unknown to Browning students and it is probable that nobody, save the recipients, had ever read the letters through in their entirety. But it is a correspondence of real importance, partly as unfolding an unguessed at and romantic episode in Browning's life and partly as giving an intimate glimpse of his activities and views between the years 1864 and 1870.

These letters, in short, must not be read as gossip, but as a serious contribution to our understanding of Browning as poet and man. His defence of *The Ring and The Book* against Miss Wedgwood's strictures is singularly illuminating, and the tenderness and what one might term the logical impatience of his character are all unconsciously revealed in these very personal and often eloquent communications.

When and how precisely Browning met Miss Wedgwood is uncertain, but it was some time during 1863 and the family tradition is that it was through his acquaintance with her eldest brother, James Mackintosh Wedgwood. Undoubtedly, as the letters disclose, it was the illness and death of this young man, who was born in April, 1834, and died in June, 1864, which ripened and deepened the friendship.

But even if the tradition be wrong, it was only natural for Julia Wedgwood to have met Robert Browning. Her family, well-to-do and of assured position, had long moved in intellectual and literary circles and had numbered amongst their friends, at one period or another, such celebrities as Wordsworth, Coleridge, Samuel Rogers, Maria Edgeworth, Thackeray, Carlyle, Macaulay, F. D. Maurice, Clough, Harriet Martineau and Mazzini. And so it was inevitable, one might almost say, that Browning, the persistent diner-out, would meet her sooner or later. But why he should have been so speedily and greatly attracted to her is another question. It is true that she was a well-read woman of vigorous opinions and a solid turn of mind—a kind of nineteenth-century blue-stocking with social leanings—, but then, many other ladies in the 'sixties were much the same. One may reasonably suppose, I think, that it was an informed discussion of his poems, of which she was already an admirer, that first drew Browning to her.

Frances Julia ("Snow") Wedgwood, born on February 6th, 1833, was then thirty. She was the eldest of the six children of Hensleigh and Frances Wedgwood and had already written two novels, one under a pseudonym and one anonymously,—they are said to be exceedingly gloomy —and had contributed to the weekly reviews. On both sides she came of distinguished ancestry: her paternal great-grandfather was Josiah Wedgwood, the potter, and her maternal grandfather was Sir James Mackintosh, the politician and philosopher, who wrote the well-known *Vindiciæ Gallicæ* in opposition to Burke's *Reflections on the French Revolution*. Her father was a philologist of parts, author of an etymological dictionary, and his sister was the wife of Charles Darwin, who was thus Miss Wedgwood's uncle by marriage. Darwin had a high opinion of his niece's ability and when, in 1861, she published in the July number of *Macmillan's Magazine* a criticism of *The Origin of Species* under the title "The Boundaries of Science," he wrote to her— I have the letter before me—"Someone has sent me 'Macmillan'; and I must tell you how much I admire your article . . . I think that you understand my book perfectly, and that I find a very rare event with my critics."

Such was the woman whom Browning met when he was fifty-one and had been a widower for between two and three years. (His wife had died on June 29th, 1861.) He was, of course, already famous, for the publication of *Men and Women* in 1855 had put the seal upon his reputation, and he was then presumably at work on *Dramatis Personæ*, which was issued in 1864. Perhaps, even, he had already started work on *The Ring and the Book*, of which we hear so much in his later letters to Miss Wedgwood; but, in any case, he was a busy and much sought-after man. And yet, despite his varied activities and the care of his son, Browning must have been essentially lonely in the first years of his widowerhood and it is plain that he found in Miss Wedgwood qualities which reminded him of his wife and a companionship which, at the outset at least, was extremely precious.

From 1863 to 1870 he wrote her thirty letters —nineteen being within about the first six months of their correspondence, when the friend-ship was in its bloom and they were meeting frequently—and she wrote him forty-two. Many of their letters are of immense length and his, in particular, range over all sorts of subjects— the death of Keats, how Mrs. Browning showed him the *Sonnets from the Portuguese,* tea with Queen Victoria, his state of health when he was composing different poems, how he would have written *Enoch Arden,* the death of Landor, a tiff with Lord Houghton, his travels in the Pyrenees, the characters of *The Ring and the Book,* and so on, and so on. They form, indeed, a fascinating record of an active life and are full of Browning's rich vitality and unexpected turn of phrase.

There is, so far as I can see, no good evidence that any of the letters from either correspondent have been lost or destroyed. If she wrote more often than he, it was largely because, in the early days, a letter from her would be answered by a visit from him. It must be admitted that she was rather a prosy and long-winded letter-writer, not unintelligent, by any means, but with a constant tendency to moralize; but for the sake of unity all her letters which answered letters from Browning or led to letters from him have been given, together with a few others which are germane. In fact, only a handful that are of no particular significance and do not carry on the story are omitted.

Needless to say, all of Browning's letters have been printed, and as they have been checked twice with the originals the text may be taken as accurate. Such words as are undecipherable or doubtful—and sometimes his writing is minute and crabbed to a disconcerting degree—have been marked.

Curiously enough, Browning's first letters to a member of the Wedgwood family, the first, at any rate, which have survived, were written to Julia's mother. They are not of much interest in themselves, but I reproduce them here for the benefit of completeness and as showing the esteem he felt for this lady. Here is the earliest:

Dear Mrs. Wedgwood,

I am engaged to-night: let me take my chance and "call": be sure I will let you be as good to me as you please a little later: I am counting upon seeing you often, indeed—being

Ever truly yours
Robert Browning

19 Warwick Crescent
Upper Westbourne Terrace, W.
Dec. 9, '63

The second letter, though undated, was evidently written in February 1864, just before Mrs. Wedgwood started on a visit to Italy:

19 Warwick Crescent,
Upper Westbourne Terr.
Monday

Dear Mrs. Wedgwood,

It may happen that I shall be unable to deliver these few notes myself this morning—in such a case, this must be my cordial good-bye.

I have begged Miss Hosmer [1] to introduce you to Gibson [1]—she being herself well worth seeing and knowing.

---

[1] Harriet Goodhue Hosmer (1830-1908) was an American sculptor who went to Rome in 1852 and studied under John Gibson, the English sculptor. "A great pet of mine and of Robert's," wrote Mrs. Browning. (*Letters of Elizabeth Barrett Browning*, 1898.)

If you give the enclosed card to Brini he will render you any service at Florence, change circular notes, no matter on what Bank, to your greatest advantage, dispatch any purchases to England &c., &c.

I give you a note to my intimate friend Miss Blagden,[1] living in a villa close by Bellosguardo —in case she can be of use, she will. If you go to Powers'[2] studio, in Via della Forana, and mention my name, he will show you everything there. I may say the same of Mademoiselle de Vauvenu—a woman of genius—opposite in the same street. Should you want a very good and cheap picture-copyist my friend Mignuty, of the Studios in Via de' Ginori, will satisfy you.

And so, cordially once again, good-bye!

Yours very faithfully,

ROBERT BROWNING

Brini will give you Miss Blagden's address: I need not say the notes are written merely to be at hand if required by any chance—not otherwise.

The introduction to Miss Blagden was appar-

---

[1] Isabella Blagden was a great friend of both the Brownings. Many of Robert Browning's letters to her have been published.

[2] Hiram Powers (1805-1873), an American sculptor, whose "Greek Slave" (1843) was apostrophized by Mrs. Browning in a sonnet.

ently not used, for it was found with the other letters. Here it is:

Dearest Isa,

This will introduce to you a very charming and accomplished Lady, the daughter of Sir James Mackintosh. I say no more, because I probably shall have written before this arrives. I know you will do any little thing in your power.

Affectionately yours ever,

Robert Browning

Feb. 8, '64

Browning, indeed, appears to have maintained a steady regard for Mrs. Wedgwood and she for him, as the correspondence depicts—Hensleigh Wedgwood, on the other hand, is not mentioned in a single letter, although he lived till 1891—; and from the fact that she asked him to dinner some two years after her daughter had requested him not to call again it might be assumed that she would have liked to see the friendship between Julia and himself revived in its old form. But that, after all, is only conjecture. And anyhow the letters must be allowed to speak in detail for themselves and to tell their own full story.

We watch a friendship beginning with enthusiastic ardour on his side and an equal responsiveness on hers. Then suddenly it crashes to the ground through her deliberate choice, and then, after an interval of several years, is built up again on a different level of emotion. It is a calmer friendship now, a friendship of letters alone, and yet, underlying the surface, there is a sort of irritability in Browning's attitude and an increasing tendency to criticize in Miss Wedgwood's. And, on her side at least, a vain regret for the vanished days and a desire to justify the action she had taken. It is as if, having lost the key, they were now resolved to express their own personalities, to come out into the open, as it were, where formerly they had wanted to enter sympathetically into each other's minds. It is all rather sad and strange, and the last letters they exchanged have a real poignancy as of a gray twilight falling upon everything.

Reading carefully through the early letters, one would be inclined to attribute the break to one of several causes. Either, as she herself wrote in so many words, she had become frightened of that mid-Victorian public opinion which was so apt to find in even the most harmless friendships between men and women a subject for talk and raised eyebrows; or, as her later letters suggest, she had been hurt by reported remarks of his about her (an accusation which Browning angrily denies); or she was getting tired of Browning and no longer felt the need of his help or the glamour of his fame; or she wanted to end the friendship before the situation became too difficult.

But whatever explanation might seem most probable, it would scarcely appear from the tone of their respective letters up to the break—save, perhaps, in some of her early ones—that his feelings were less fervent that were hers. Of course, the reserves and phraseology of seventy years ago make it hard to judge from letters what people were really thinking, but even allowing for the feminine attitude of those days, which carried reticence to the point of absurdity and covered up normal reactions by a flood of sententious generalities, that is the conclusion to which one might have come.

And yet, apparently, it would have been wrong. Doubtless she *was* affected by what people said to her and doubtless she *was* wounded by his rumoured observations, but the real reason for the break went deeper. It is made clear enough in a letter from a woman friend of hers, Julia M. Stirling,[1] written, in answer to a letter from Miss Wedgwood, on March 5th, 1865, after her decision had been taken. I quote some sentences from it:

"Judge what I must have felt in receiving your letter and enclosure this morning. I know what a mournful death-knell it must seem to you. But yet we can rejoice together that since it had to be rung there is no *jar* in it to his mind. With all the evident pain he feels in giving up what has been precious to him, there is not even a *reserve* in his mind of reproach for you—and it is transparent throughout that he knew this separation must come: he too felt you were both in an untenable position; but as you had pointed to it he could hardly withdraw till you showed him you desired it. Such a friendship the longer it is indulged, the more absorbing it becomes in the nature of things—and now your heart must be torn out by the roots. I am so touched when he says 'Certainly you are right in being sure that I understand you!'—For it shows me what a real effort you must have made in your appeal to him to conceal the fact that your heart had betrayed you. If he guesses the truth, he certainly most

---

[1] Miss Stirling was an old friend of the family and lived at Falmouth. She survived Miss Wedgwood.

honorourably ignores it—and makes the path easy to you which you now have chosen."

Which leads one to ask, *Did* Browning guess the truth and was he not, perhaps, a little relieved that she, herself, had ended a friendship which threatened to grow embarrassing? After all, he was a keen psychologist and his readiness to accede to her request not to visit her—one can imagine how very different his tone would have been a few months before—does almost suggest that he had seen the danger-signal. And yet, again, a later letter of his appears to show that he had been hurt and bewildered by her action and could think of no valid reason why their former close friendship should not have continued. We must just leave it at that, always remembering that a good psychologist may be a bad psychologist where his own interests are concerned.

It is a moot point when the revelation of a confidence may be justifiable, but in all the circumstances it has been thought wiser and fairer to state the facts than to leave anything in dubiety. Whatever Browning's original feelings may have been—and that is far from clear—, it is obvious that she had come finally to mean nothing to him but a friend, while it is equally obvious that he had come to be regarded by her as something more. Things being what they were, her unselfishness was admirable; while her courage in keeping Browning in the dark about her feelings and thus not putting him in a false position was heroic. But there was a certain bleakness in her resolve which, I dare say, was partly temperamental and partly in the spirit of the times. Her woman friend, in another part of that letter from which I have already quoted, had remarked with dismal and tactless finality, "Do not think of *Hope*. That is not to be dreamt of for years," and one cannot but feel that such a sentiment accorded very well with Julia Wedgwood's own.

There is no proof that Browning and Miss Wedgwood ever met after 1865 or corresponded after 1870, but the impression he left upon her was evidently powerful and lasting, for when she published her best-known book, *The Moral Ideal*, in 1888—it has been called a sort of prose representation of Browning's own philosophy—, she dedicated it to "An Old Friend," who, as she subsequently informed Professor C. H. Herford of Manchester University, was Robert Browning. The Professor, who had known her for thirty years, revealed this in the Memoir of Miss

Wedgwood which he affixed to her posthumous *Life* of Josiah Wedgwood, 1915, in these words:

"It may now be made known that the 'Old Friend,' as she told the editor in confidence ten years ago, was Robert Browning."

And in another way, a negative way, one may gauge the strength of the hold he had upon her memory. Apparently she could not bring herself to write about him and though she collected into a volume essays she had contributed to such periodicals as the *Spectator* and the *Contemporary Review* on people who had influenced her, there is no essay on Browning. And yet both as a teacher and as a person he had influenced her enormously.

Browning died on December 12th, 1889, at the age of seventy-seven, and, as was to be expected, Miss Wedgwood survived him for many years, dying on November 26th, 1913, at the age of eighty. Those who remember her recall a very deaf (deafness was an almost life-long infirmity with her) and rather formidable old lady, whose manner was severe and whose mind was fixed on higher things. She possessed, as one writer on her says, "a passion for righteousness," but though her conversation was far from light, yet she was a brilliant and copious talker and had a genuine love of art. For many years she rose at four every morning in order to get her day's writing done before breakfast, and altogether there was a good deal of the stoic, and perhaps of the martinet, in her character.

She died in London, where she had passed most of her life, and was buried in Staffordshire. I have read many of her obituary notices, and though they are respectful in tone, they are, with few exceptions, the kind of obituary notices, inaccurate and perfunctory, which are written about people who have outlived their fame. Not that she ever had much fame, but that, in her middle years, she did fill a distinct, small niche in the moral, rather than the artistic, world of the last century. She was a typical product of her age, learned, earnest, inspired by a somewhat arid cosmic morality. Like so many of her contemporaries she yearned to systematize the universe and to bring religion, philosophy and science into line. She had the talents and the force of character to arouse respect in every one, but few of those who knew her can have dreamt that, hidden from prying eyes, she cherished in secret this moving and very human correspondence.

As the shadows of old age deepened about her did she, in the quiet of her solitude, read over

these letters occasionally and re-live once more
those exciting days when a note from Browning,
to be followed, maybe, by a call, would brighten
existence and give it a thrill which serious
thoughts somehow could not quite manage to
give it? I feel that she probably did, but that
she regarded such readings as moments of weakness. There was that anti-vivisection pamphlet
to read—she was a convinced anti-vivisectionist
and left several thousand pounds of her consider-
able fortune to the cause—and there was so
much else to do. Duty came first, and whatever
one may think of her letters as letters, they do,
in the light of what we know, reveal her integrity
and prove that not even her idol, Browning,
could ever have swerved her one hair's-breadth
from the course she had mapped out.

I am much indebted to my friend, Mr. Maurice Buxton Forman, the erudite Editor of
Keats's Letters, for making the great majority of
the Notes and the Index to these Letters. Also
the list of Miss Wedgwood's books. Nobody
could have done the work more capably and he
has added decisively to the value of the book.
Moreover, his specialized knowledge has been at
my service throughout and he has helped me in
various ways. I cannot thank him sufficiently.

RICHARD CURLE

Saturday, May 14th, 1864,
Cumberland Place

MY DEAR MR. BROWNING,

You have shown so much kind interest in us, that I am glad to write and tell you that my Brother,[1] though not any better, and never to be so in this world according to all probability, seems now a little further removed from the end than I thought when I saw you last. There is now almost no suffering and we hope this may continue so that there is nothing to prevent our indulging the wish, which in some illnesses might be so cruel, to keep him for some little time,—perhaps weeks, I hardly dare to hope for months. —The knowledge of your sympathy has been a great comfort to me.

[2] Your own unparalleled loss [3] must dwarf in comparison every other separation, but I believe it is just those who have experienced the worst of

---

[1] James Mackintosh Wedgwood, b. April, 1834, d. June, 1864.

[2] Both Miss Wedgwood's and Browning's letters have been re-paragraphed where desirable and, to some extent, repunctuated.

[3] Elizabeth Barrett Browning died at Casa Guidi, Florence, on the 29th of June, 1861.

that terrible wrench, who can also feel the most for those who undergo a lighter form of it. You were an old friend to me long before I saw you, so that it does not seem unnatural to me to express the deep sympathy which I long have had for such a loss as yours, and which is now brought out afresh, with the thought of all such separation, as the dark shadows close around us. But there is nothing reciprocal in the way I knew you, and I need hardly say I want no response to this.

I shall be at home tomorrow from one to half past two (about the time you have called before, I think) and indeed that is always my time for being at home, and if not very busy it would always give me great pleasure to see you. But I hope you and your son [1] are enjoying this lovely Whitsunstide in the country somewhere, for I hope you have not learnt to despise our English spring.

Ever your sincere friend,
JULIA WEDGWOOD

MY DEAR MISS WEDGWOOD,

I shall only repeat, though unnecessarily, that if I can ever be found capable of the least use to

---

[1] Robert Wiedemann Barrett Browning, b. 9 March, 1849.

you, it will make me glad and grateful indeed. I daresay that I have managed to give you a notion that the distance between your house and mine is formidable:[1] the time of the journey from door to door cannot exceed twenty minutes, by railway.

Faithfully yours ever,
ROBERT BROWNING

Saturday, June 25th, 1864,
1 Cumberland Place, N.W.

DEAR AND KINDEST FRIEND,

It brings me as near to a pleasure as anything can in this terrible moment to write to you and tell you that all is peacefully over and that the spirit we have been watching for so long has passed out of the range of our small vision. It was yesterday at 3 o'clock without pain or struggle of any kind. I have lost a Brother [2]—it seems so natural to write it to you, you who have been to me a Barnabas in such a sorrow as I trust no human being is called upon twice to endure in this life. It seems strange to say so much with-

---

[1] Browning was living at 19 Warwick Crescent, Upper Westbourne Terrace, W., and Miss Wedgwood at 1 Cumberland Place, Regent's Park, N.W.

[2] See Note 1, page 1.

out fear of misconception, but I go on to say
more, and express to you a part of the consolation you have given me. It is that while I have
shivered in this cold darkness without a glimmer
of hope, or with only a glimmer, I have felt with
you in the presence of one who could bear a loss
so much greater than mine because the remnant
of life was an insignificant break in an intercourse not more secure in the Past than in the
Future. I knew the tone of hope, of life, could
not exist apart from *that* knowledge, I knew what
a wreck your life would be, if you could not discern an opening, where I saw only darkness.

I suppose this moonlight trust is all that can
be attained by those who walk on the night side
of the world, but to them it is a witness to the unseen sun, when nothing else can be. At this
solemn moment it seems easy to go on, rather it
seems impossible to stop, till I have said all I
want to say. I think it has been indeed implied
in every word of mine to you, but I wish to say it
distinctly. A woman who has taken the initia-
tive in a friendship with a man, as I have done
with you, has either lost all right feeling or has
come to a very definite decision on the issue of
all such friendships. I have told you what your
intercourse has been to me, and I am sure you

hardly needed to be told, for it was sufficiently obvious. But precious as it is, I could—not perhaps at this painful moment, but in due time— bear to give it up without unreasonable pain, for any reason but one, for any good reason at least. That one exception would be if your kind heart checked you in any approach to me with a fear of the consequences to myself. I have never seen the slightest tinge of such a fear, but I am made cowardly by a life of much estrangement and suffering; I prefer the scorn which falls on those who say too much, to the price which may have to be paid by those who say too little. I could look back on our concluded intercourse without any bitterness if it were simply ended by the natural course of events, calling you to more equal friendships, but it would be bitter, oh very bitter, to feel that you had drawn back from mistaken kindness to me, that you had feared to inflict a pain against which I am shielded by the deliberate decision of my mature life.

Again and eagerly I declare that I have never seen any approach to this in your mind, it is the natural suggestion of my own. It seems to me almost an unnecessary protest, but that almost tears away all my scruple in the strangeness of what I write. I cannot afford to lose any more

kindness and sympathy, it would be the harder to
lose it through kindness. I write to you in the
awful stillness that follows that last look. I can
only speak as spirit to spirit. Nay, why do I
justify myself, for I have no fears of your misconception. I know that the strangeness would
strike anyone else, but I believe it will seem quite
natural to you. I believe that you, from the first,
have consciously supplied that place which has
for some time been empty to me! That it may
be so for a time is my utmost hope; when it
ceases to become natural or easy, do not try to
continue it, I have a fine ear for any strain in intercourse. Remember then that the knowledge
of you was a cordial in this swoon of life that is
not likely to recur—that I had such a consolation
exactly at the moment when I imperiously
needed it.

I shall very soon wish to see you again, and
perhaps you will let me summon you. You will
not wonder to hear that my mother [1] is physically
worn out, but I think it is the best thing for her
mind. When I can see any one, it will be you.

Ever yours very gratefully,

JULIA WEDGWOOD

---

[1] Frances Wedgwood, daughter of the Rt. Hon. Sir James Mackintosh, Bart., M.P.; she died on the 15th of May, 1889.

MY DEAR FRIEND,

You know that I feel for you from my heart. Three years ago, in this very week, I lost my own soul's companion.[1] If I have any instinct or insight,—if I can retain and rightly reason upon the rare flashes of momentary conviction that come and go in the habitual dusk and doubt of one's life—(and this in spite of a temper perhaps offensively and exaggeratedly inclined to dispute authoritative tradition, and all concessions to the mere desires of the mind)—if the result of all this can no more be disputed as *something*—or even, as *much*—than pretended to be *everything,* then I dare believe that you and that I shall recover what we have lost: I am not given to hope, nor self-flattery: and my belief is a verȳ composite and unconventional one, and I myself am most surprised at detecting its strength in the unforeseen accidents of life which throw one upon one's resources and show them for what they exactly are. I am sure you will one day feel such a support, even if it should seem uncertain now—and meanwhile I tell you conscientiously how it is with me.

What you say (after what makes me write

---

[1] See Note 3, page 1.

this) respecting our intercourse—your feeling and mine—on that, too, I must write a little—the impulse being to write much, because very many earnest thoughts are excited by your letter —and while each of them is, in some sort, proper for you to hear, all of the multitude would confuse us in speaking and hearing. As good a way will be to confine oneself to just the simple facts —for these are suggestive also and will reply to questions not immediately applicable to them. I shall tell you then, that I do understand you, and know that you understand me. Be assured that your friendship has been always precious to me, and that while I live it will be most precious: it would have been so at any time in the past,— which I say, when you speak of my sympathy having been a "consolation" to you: the circumstances under which I have come to know you may certainly have so operated that, in the meeting of our hands, mine has seemed somewhat to lift, rather than be lifted by, yours. But that has been only a chance—and any day you would help me as much. Simply, I value your friendship for me, as you shall know, if you will but wait: and it already seems useless to tell you that wherever I may be of the slightest good to you, it will be my pride and privilege when you count on me.   And now—no more assurances of this kind from me, nor, surely, any need for them that you will ever feel.

I shall leave this when I call to-morrow in the hope of hearing that you all bear up and strengthen each other in this emergency, as is right.

God bless you, dear friend!

Yours affectionately ever,

ROBERT BROWNING

1, Cumberland Place, N.W.
Sunday, June 27th, [1864][1]

DEAREST FRIEND,

Your letter has been a gleam into the darkness of my mind to-day—perhaps the more steady a gleam in that region, because as you say yourself, it is the utterance of a mind opposed to all authoritative forms of traditional belief, such as most rest on at moments like these, but which have no support for me.   I prize the intense conviction of the minds which can rest in these forms, but I prize more—at least, I find more possibility of approach towards—those minds which can retain the hope of the future amid the

---

[1] Dates in square brackets were added by Miss Wedgwood.

complex suggestions of intellectual doubt, and the distrust of that mere *wish* which forms so large a part of the faith of most people. What opposite needs converge to this desire of an Immortality!—you need it, I know, for the continuation of an intercourse which only needed this element for perfection, while I feel—But I will not let my thoughts revert for a moment to the mistakes of an irrevocable Past. I can rest on the present while it is enriched by intercourse with you. I trust that mistakes will not come in here, that our communion may find its limits in the natural action of your many other claims, and not in any withering influence from me; but I dread myself, for I know there is in me an exacting spirit that dries up all the love and kindness which it needs so terribly.

I take you at your word, I do want this bond to life now, for the time. You must remember that it is on my side essentially an *old* friendship. And if, as I think in spite of your words, there is something fugitive in it, if I fear that the mere accident (as I feel it for all its influence on my feelings for you) of your being a man and my being a woman is inimical to its long existence in this *personal* form, you must remember that what I had before I knew you, perhaps the larger part of your mind, I should still have after our intercourse had ceased. But it is very welcome to me that you think differently. Will you come and see me on Thursday or Friday, and let me know when?

I ventured to show your letter to my mother: without explanations she might have made the natural mistake which I wished to guard against. She was startled at the unusual course I had taken, hers is a mind to perceive very clearly the many objections to it, but as she saw I had lost nothing in your eyes by it, she was satisfied. Wednesday is the dreary day that is to remind us of the mere garment of the spirit that has passed from us. I find a peculiar need for forgetting that part of it! Farewell, dear friend.

Yours ever,

JULIA W.

June 27, '64

DEAR FRIEND,

I will call on Thursday at about 4 o'clock. When you most feel the inadequacy of the best we can know on the matter in your mind now, ask yourself fairly how it would be with you if you could suddenly attain to absolute conviction about it, in the sense of your desire,—if the whole relations of this world would not be changed to you, and life, as you now find it prescribed, rendered no longer possible: one may assume, then, that for probational or educational purposes to ourselves, more than the yearning we *have*, and the corroborative facts which, by various processes, I think we *may* have, is inexpedient and out of the present harmony: if you object that one might also reverse the experiment and see in like manner the whole scheme of our life changed by attaining to the opposite conviction of the nothingness of this hope,—I answer that this theory involves, I must think, a crime against humanity, while the other is consistent with wisdom and benevolence—therefore the likelier hypothesis.

Last night I was talking with a friend who read aloud a passage from Dr. Newman's *Apology* [1] in which he says that "he is as convinced of the existence of God"—an individual, not an external force merely—"as of his own existence." I believe he deceives himself and that no sane man has ever had, with mathematical exactness, equal conviction on those two points—

---

[1] John Henry Newman (1801-1890). His *Apologia Pro Vita Sua*, replying to an attack by Charles Kingsley in "Macmillan's Magazine," appeared in 1864.

though the approximation to equality may be in any degree short of that: and looking at the practical effects of belief, I should expect that it would be so: I can see nothing that comes from absolute contact, so to speak, between man and God, but everything in all variety from the greater or less distance between the two. When anyone tells me that he *has* such a conviction, I look at a beggar who holds the philosopher's stone according to his profession. Do you see the bearing of all this as I seem to see it? How, remaining beggars—or poor, at least—we may at once look for the love of those to whom we give our mite, though we throw it into the darkness where they only *may* be: fortunately the experiment on our faith is never a very long one.

I am glad that you showed my letter to Mrs. Wedgwood. You know well what is the way of the world with any exceptional mode of proceeding: if one wears a white tie instead of a black one, or calls at a house at 10: rather than 5: P.M. —it has something to say and smile about. It is for you to determine when it is right that I should see you. I thought myself too plainly a sort of tombstone, to be scribbled over when so many blank walls spread on every side: yet a friend of yours and mine did, out of fun, write a silly name

·13·

on me some months ago, which was read and repeated by various people: to be sure, it came
rather of following than departing from the ways
of the world, in this instance—seeing that being
bidden by our hostess to take a lady down to
dinner, I did so—and when the lady told me she
would not sit by so and so, I let her sit away from
him—whence all this! All I say is, or repeat
rather, I shall be happy to have your confidence
and your friendship: and when you talk of what
may be "inimical" to it, and of the chances which
are natural, I can only remind you that circumstances guard me against many of these—that
the veriest weathercock may *rust* and hardly turn
again—and that I see a plain line to the end of
my life on which I shall walk, unless an accident
stop all walking,—I shall not diverge, at least.

Do not let us talk more about this: but, once
for all, and for truth's sake, and because you refer to a doubt again,—believe in the complete
equality of our relation, and that, from the beginning of my acquaintance with you, I was
aware, in proportion to my knowledge of you,
that it might greatly interest and advantage me:
but of course, it is not, because I may know
where pictures are, that I knock at the gallery
door daily: now you have thrown it open, let me

tell you I like pictures and do not stand before them merely from a wish to wipe the dust from their frames.

And now, this is a letter! and I do not write letters,—and I shall not, if you please, write many such, for we can and will talk about everything that interests us: and there is lightness in this, because if you take my arm you must keep my pace, and HOPE: do you know, a phrenologist told me when I was about sixteen that I had absolutely no hope at all in the head of me —and so it really was in those days. But I do think I see light at the far end of the passage. Not that I should like you at all to stand in my place so far on from the entry: you should *live*, step by step, *up* to the proper place where the pin-point of light is visible: nothing is to be overleaped, the joy no more than the sorrow, and then, your part done, God's may follow, and will, I trust. I am sure you already see much to do, and the comfort of it. Care, too, for your health, in mere fairness to those you love—such sadness grows out of mistake about their interest there! There are people that should know better who hold one's glass heart in their hand, throw it up and catch it again with the pavement under-neath. You will not do so: let me find that on Thursday and know me ever for

Yours affectionately,

R. B.

MY DEAR FRIEND,

Can you let me call on you to-morrow at about 3, instead of 4, o'clock, as I had appointed? I shall suppose so unless I hear otherwise.

My whole sympathy is with you to-day as you must know—as yours would have been with me this day [1] three years ago: yet I shall go out to-day. It would be too foolish telling friends in effect "there is a difference in my thoughts to-day," when there is none.

God bless you,

Yours affectionately,

R. BROWNING

June 29, '64

1 Cumberland Place, N. W.,
Wednesday night

DEAR FRIEND,

Any time in the afternoon I shall be equally glad to see you. I do not wonder you shrink

---

[1] The third anniversary of Mrs. Browning's death.

· 16 ·

from any peculiar sanctification of anniversaries which shall seem to exclude the rest of the year, which must to you be one long anniversary. How infinite the possibilities are of human desire! I cannot conceive a greater loss than yours, and yet I am quite sure it excluded some of the pain I am feeling now. We have each our own nadir; when I can look up, I suppose we shall find we have each our own zenith too.

I am afraid you are too sanguine in expecting to avoid the "graffiti" you speak of, but the next shower will wash them out. You will be glad to hear that my mother has not suffered in health from the event [1] of today.

Ever yrs,

J. W.

Leith Hill Place,
July 23rd, 1864

I wonder if you will be surprised at any letter coming so soon—No, I do not think you will. I feel as if I were safe from surprise with you. Is it a rash hope? I live upon it for the present, at any rate. I have just come in from walking in these woods where I have walked any time these

---

[1] The funeral of her son, James Mackintosh Wedgwood.

fifteen years. I stopped continually to ask myself if it was really *I* who was walking in them, where were all the companions that had clung to that woman of past years so closely, she is startled to find them gone—the regrets, the wishes, the weariness of life. Are they all really gone? will they not return?—Surely I think they must—but meantime what a strange wonder, what a foretaste of immortality to feel oneself without them. What most undoes my sense of identity is the loss of that one desire that bent all my inward life like an unseen magnet. I look round me today at the shrubs and the distant hills as if I should find some change in *them*, that I had ceased to feel, "Oh Earth, release me!"

Is it possible that I do not still pull against that chain? and that it is only because a fellow-creature—not spotlessly perfect, by any means —tells me that my absence makes a hole in his life, that I am willing, oh more than willing, to keep my foothold here, while he cares to have me? Ah, something tells me that my faithful companion will return to me, that I shall have to live, when my life has lost that fragrance of being *something to you*, but it will not be as it has been.

One thing, I know, could make me regret that I had ever known you, if I missed anything ungracious or ignoble in your life, but nothing else. Oh, I hope your wife hears my thoughts as I write to you! Is it not a marvellous thing that *we* hear no thoughts?—only the poor hortus sciens of words reaches our sense, while the growing garden is inaccessible. Surely it is not so hereafter, and if ever one human soul can come near another, it must be when such a feeling contains them both, as ours for you.

With what a wonderful fearlessness of misconception I am writing to you! I did not think such utterance was possible while we were clothed in flesh, but with you I have invincibly a sense of that emergence being past. I search my spirit in vain for anything that I would hide from you. I do indeed find much that would oppose itself to you, as there is that in you which I question and criticize, but nothing that would separate us. I am not feminine, they say. Well, it is true for good as well as for evil. That sounds arrogant, and if ever God meant to teach any of his creatures humility, certainly it is *my* lesson—but it is true. Your wife always seems to me so eminently a woman, the maternal, the conjugal relation seem necessary parts of her character, one feels they were the expressions of herself. With me, all the relations of life are unfortunate, and I do not feel that it just so happens because the beloved and honoured ones with whom I share them are what they are—but because of something in me which grates against all the material bonds of life. My sphere is the intercourse of spirit with spirit—there I breathe a pure air, there indeed I am not meant to linger long, or life would not be to me the discipline I suppose it is to every one,—but there is my home, and this is my excuse for this fearlessness towards you.

Oh, when you said those words "I lost" what a thrill went through me!—I believe you. I shall believe you, if you seem ever so much to change to me, for I should know it was not you that had changed, but I that had ended so much sooner than you expected, and left you no choice but to quit the tiny place. If I dwell so much on the thought, if our intercourse seems on my part one perpetual farewell,[1] it is not that in *you* I see any sign of leavetaking, my liberal guest, but

---

[1] Miss Wedgwood's spelling was generally correct, but in writing this word she alternated between "farewell" and "farewel." She also seems to have had some difficulty in deciding between *ei* and *ie* in such words as grief and chief. The other few lapses in her letters may fairly be regarded as slips of the pen, and, as they are not in any way characteristic, her occasional mistakes have been corrected and printed without comment.

that my love is inseparably entangled with fear, the two chords vibrate together. All love has been passion with me, and it is a simple translation of that phrase to say that at one time or other, all love has proved a scourge. Then, with you, I am continually pleading to God—Oh let it be separation, let it be loss! don't make it misconception, bitterness and that wrath that works like madness in the brain!

Could I bear never to see you again? Yes, from the bottom of my soul. Could I bear to feel angry with you? I suppose we poor human beings mean something when we say we cannot bear what we do bear, I suppose I should say in that case with poor Heine

Und ich hab' es doch ertragen
Aber frage mir nur nicht wie! [1]

And if you say that in this anticipatory self-torment I am addressing a Setebos [2] rather than

---

[1] Heine's lines in his *Buch der Lieder*, 1827, from which Miss Wedgwood quotes, have been translated—

First methought in my affliction
I can never bear this woe,—
Yet I did—strange contradiction!
How I did, ne'er seek to know.

He is said to have written them at a ball, referring to a very tight shoe.

[2] Browning's "Caliban upon Setebos" was published in *Dramatis Personæ*, 1864. Setebos was the god of the Patagonians, thought by Caliban to live in the moon and to have made mankind for his amusement.

a Father—I only reply that I judge for no one but myself. I rejoice to contemplate love that is not steeped in pain such as you have known, but for myself I feel as if that were no part of the intentions of Heaven. My hope will not rise above the level of my memory—not indeed that there is not space, but she is tired and moves no more into the unknown. And so it comes that I find myself imploring bearable pain, not pleasure. Oh what different dimensions there are in one's wishes! First, for you, that you may live unfalteringly up to your highest ideal—that fills up all the space you occupy in my heart—then, that sorrow may keep far from you, and last and least of all, length without breadth, that you may continue to me what you are. Perhaps this is vain cowardice, perhaps our friendship will be the streak of foreign light which I think falls into most lives—but I cannot rest on a perhaps. I want to have no more disappointment. I want to live in tents. Bear with this distrust, not of you, but of Fate, who will have to change all her treatment of me, if she leaves me you!

You asked me for my photograph, to which this letter is a very complete answer. O my friend, what unique trust is in my soul, that it can thus unveil itself to you: admitting you into the place where I thought I was alone with God. Sunday.—do I wish I was back in Cumberland Place today? you shall guess. Shall you be tired if you have many of these letters from me? I think you will be tested. I rather think you are an impatient personage, and that it will be good for you to read many effusions from such a tiresome person as yours,

F. J. W.

Next week at Lady Inglis's
Milton Bryan,
Woburn,
Beds.
that is to say, after tomorrow.

19 Warwick Crescent,
July 25, '64

You make me very happy, and could not do it in any other way. You know I understand you: also that if I believe you, as it is easy to do, there is all honour implied to you by believing. I know that, besides what else you are, you are truthful and generous, with the courage proper to these. If I did not so feel, and so understand, I am good enough to be able, and easily, to return you your gifts and say they were not meant

·23·

for me, as an honest streetsweeper would, on finding that you had given gold for the silver coin, that is already too unusual a largess: if I were vain, I mean, and weak and selfish only, I would not take this gold of you, when silver compliment, or even sympathy, would be enough.

But, dearest friend, if, *since* you choose to care thus for me, I can be sure of satisfying you just when [1] you feel uncertain of the effects of your care—I *shall* "last" at the lowest that one can say. I do not turn round, as I might, and tell you, it is *you* who will find me out, one day, and be ashamed and sorry when the illusion goes: I don't think that: my way, too, is the "cynical" rather than the sentimental—I shall tell you the truth, if I can, as I have so far told you the exact truth: my past life,—how long compared to yours!—is of use here: you know that, without needing to be better than my fellows, I am lifted by past experiences above the temptation to be false and selfish and vain in such a relation as ours—do I want you to wear like a ring round my neck-tie, as the fashion is?—I am older than to care to look fine *so*. There would be real matters for regret, if I tried to find the real ob-

---

[1] This word may be "where."

stacles at all likely to seriously inconvenience us.

But don't think of them now—it is my vice and plague to do exactly what a friend of mine did on Saturday while you, maybe, were writing your letter. I was at his house—he disappeared mysteriously—his wife explained "That microscope you wished to see, he is preparing something"—at last, in he came, "Such a disappointment! There was only one of the insects in the *aquarium*—one that I was anxious to show you—I got it at last—well under the glass —when, I thought I would give one screw more and—it was dead!"—I am apt to give "one screw more" and squeeze to death what yields most pleasure, turning and trying and torturing: yet, with this old habit against me, I entertain no doubt or fear of the future with us two. How shall misconception come, and "anger" and the rest?

You see the disjointed way of writing—I am unused to this way of direct transfusion of souls. Understand what you can—and you will.

You know the difficulties will begin soon enough: my visits will seem importunate, be remarked on, the usual course of things must be looked for. And then, *you,* yourself, now, let me speak plainly—keep you in mind, for justice' sake, exactly what my claims are—arising from your own free gift, but understood in their largest sense,—and do not let them presume to obstruct what may, ought to be claims paramount: don't cut, in that royal way, your palm-tree to the heart, that the poor traveler you delight to honor may have a draught of palm wine, "after which" says Xenophon, "the whole tree withers." A better than I, God knows, should have the whole palm tree in its season. There, that's said. Meantime, grow and be happy, and let me sit under the branches to my day's end, come what will.

"Tiresome person"—yes, and I shall bear your tiresomeness. Is this your fan's tap which completes the grace of a lady's gift? It does not slay me, anyhow. Forgive all that is stupid in all this, which I dare not re-read; and only mind the main truth that

I am ever yours,
R. B.

Milton Bryan,
Tuesday, July 26th. [1864.]

I was pleased to have the composition of an obscure author to study this morning. I hope I shall have many such contributions to the *Epistola Obscurorum Virorum.* I think I understand this last perfectly. Thank you for taking me at my word. It is a compliment to which women are not much accustomed, more's the pity. Yes I believe I *am* true. It was so horrible to me to find mȳ attitude towards you looked upon as it was for a time, that this infused something of hesitation towards you—if one who loved and knew me well (neither my father or mother) could hint "a fear left basking [1] over a wall, etc."—the doubt was sometimes in my mind whether this aspect was possible from your point of view, but thank God that is past.

You will repay me, will you not, for that glimpse of Hell you will entirely trust me?— I have forgiven the other, it cannot be quite forgotten but I see that the fault was in my speaking a language strange to their ear in which many misunderstandings were possible without blame. But it was not strange to you, dear friend, ȳou knew your grey hairs wd protect you from that kind of thing, if nothing else did!—you see I will not let you escape from the contrast of my exultant youth!—Ah, I wish I were young. But at least I am a great deal younger than you, and

---

[1] This word is not quite clear.

will not surrender one iota of that advantage. I shall have many a day's work to do upon this earth, when you have quitted it, and must make haste and get out of you all I want to get it done in time.

How many things remind me of you now! My Aunt today, speaking of her past happiness —the passionate love whose embers give her all the warmth she needs—described it in the words of Lady Rachel Russell "it wanted nothing of Heaven but immortality." With whom were my thoughts then? You would have laughed if you could sometimes have overheard our conversations about you. The first time she saw you, she caught a glimpse of you at some pictures, she scolded me because your appearance did not satisfy her. "Well, I saw your Mr B. and I don't think he looks poetical at all."—"No, I don't think he does, particularly" said I, trying to propitiate her. "Well then, why do you admire his poems? How can a man write poetry who is not poetical? I don't know how that can be." "But that is very foolish. You confess he is not poetical, and yet you admire his poems."—I thought it hard to be called to account for your looks!

This is a house where I should not venture to

open a newspaper on Sunday to save something much more precious than my life. I always feel muzzled here, and overflow in pen-and-ink, to the oppression of my friends, who however are not obliged to flow back again. Strait is the gate, and narrow is the way, is impressed on one's soul at every step, and I feel as if my hoop, tho' not a very large one, wd hardly get through. —Well, narrow is the spirit that cannot bear with narrowness! And in truth I sometimes doubt whether you or they are right. I say *you* in a very wide sense, all you who hold that one may fetch fire from Heaven or Hell so that one's torch burns brightly. No, I know you don't exactly say that, but the artist mind demands intensity above every thing else, and there are some things you can't set square with that Gospel. I cd be intense enough, if I might hate and scorn. That thirst for the Infinite in the Finite has been the source of so much disturbance in my life.—Love—I wanted to put that everywhere, to fill every cup to the brim with it, and it was simply annoying and inconvenient to others to find them all so full. So I have come to look upon your idea as for me, a temptation of the Devil. What you charge me not to do for you, I have been trying to do for everybody

(Xenophon's palm-wine) and my Ten thousand did not want my wine very often.

Ah no, dear friend, do not you be afraid of or for me. I am sheltered in the happiness of a very definite allegiance in my own house, which I would not surrender under a greater pressure than losing the luxury of our intercourse. It would be a loss—but not an intolerable one—oh, I have said all that before. But in truth I do not think I shall be tired.[1] You saw me under the perturbation of that insult, as I must call it though it came from a noble nature, but that was something purely accidental and passing, and will not return. A life of silence as mine is [2] (though it is so possible to forget it with you) breeds a peculiar indifference towards the opinion of the world. I know not whether it is for good or for evil, but one who never *over-hears*, cares little for and knows little of that surface current of opinion which expresses itself in slight remark. The result is that I simply omit that borderland of the *fitting* from my territory, and try to settle the question between right and wrong—and happily, it will be always

---

1 This may be "tried."
2 A reference to her deafness: see Introduction.

easy while I have parents whose wishes bring in that element.

As for my letters, I may pour them out without any fear of entangling *you* in annoying gossip. Your son, I suppose, is hardly old enough yet to represent "the world" in that point of view? You need not write to me as often as I to you, but you must rather often send me a letter if it is only to say "We are well." One grows morbidly fearful in such sad times as we have gone through. A superstitious pang went through my heart as I opened a chance book upon Burke's lamentation over the death of his only son! I have a superstition which you must learn to put up with that I can prevent evils by speaking of them and fearing them. Alas! it has sometimes failed me.

I have changed my plans and leave here tomorrow; my address for the next fortnight is below, but do not think you are bound to make use of it—oh no, I will not give in to those stupid forms.

Ever yr,
J. W.

The Crag,
Maenporth, Falmouth

It happens, however, that I *shall* "make use of
your address" at once, though I needn't—because I rather need a pin-head-sized drop of palm
wine just now, being out of sorts on various
accounts and perhaps no-accounts, so I hold up
the tip of my finger to catch it as having a right,
please observe!   And now, please further observe, I am "feminine," if you are not, and bent
consequently on having the last word about that
palm-wine—and being as clearheaded to-day as
the enforcedly temperate usually are, I shall tell
you exactly what it was I meant—not quite what
you fancy—that I would not have you give away
more in your generosity than you may need to
account for, hereafter, in your justice, when
some husbandman from a far country arrives and
wants his whole palm tree: in other words,—no,
there shall be other silences.

And now, the good of saying this is, that I can
add with a safe conscience, "what wine you can
afford, my own friend, I am quite thirsty enough
for, and not a drop shall be spilt, do believe!"
And then—do you want some the uses of my
age?   well, I *know*,—shall I say?—the signs
and tokens, by this time, and how palm-wine is

not proof-spirit, of which I am not without the experience of certain thimble-fulls: oh, the *vivandières* will press *le petit verre* on us old grey *moustaches* "for love," if we flaunt a *chevron* or two and have arms presented to us by the sentinels! And now, doing you this homage, let my own turn come, nor let mistake be feared, when I tell the pure truth that you are most dear to me, and will be ever so. I can live in very various spheres of activity, like those insects that people dry up and keep for years in a pill-box— something that had the sea to swim in once: I can't get *that* again, but any globule of your palm-wine will set me free within its circumference, to legs' content; and it is far more likely that you will decide "Enough of kicking and capering—back to your box now!"—than that I shall object,—(in the phrase of begging letter writers and so not inappropriate here!)—to partially recovering the use of my precious limbs.

As to what you say of my Devil's Gospel,—I cannot disagree with you altogether. It is one of the facts of my experience that one limits sorrowfully one's pretension to influence other people for good: I live more and more—what am I to write?—for God not man—I don't care what men think now, knowing they will never think my thoughts; yet I need increasingly to tell *the truth*——for whom? Is it that *I* shall be the better, the larger for it, have the fairer start in next life, the firmer stand? Is it pure selfishness or the obedience to a natural law? How funnily and contemptibly one does good, when that happens! I had, two days ago, letters from the father,——no, the husband of that unwise lady who came for my decision about Sludge,[1]——and from the girl herself: he "is to be indebted to me all the days of his life," and she "has indeed been saved from fearful misery!"——By what?—— And yet, by what, once, did I *not* try, with the utmost of my soul's strength, to demonstrate that out of figs and grapes could come neither thorns nor thistles——and all in vain!

I stay here till Monday certainly——the stupid absence of my publisher [2] whom I have to see may even detain me longer, but I hope not.

I shall go to Wimbledon presently to meet

---

[1] "Mr. Sludge, the Medium," i.e. David Dunglass Home, or Hume, whom Browning detected cheating. Later Home called on the poet at his house in Dorset Street and was ejected.

[2] "My publisher" at this date may have been Edward Chapman, who retired from the firm of Chapman and Hall in 1864, the year in which his house published *Dramatis Personæ*. *The Ring and the Book*, Browning's next publication, did not come out until 1868, when it was published by Smith Elder and Company.

Jenny Lind [1] at LY. Westmorland's: do you remember our sitting behind her empty stool at Made. Schwabe's? [1] I don't greatly take to that our most religious and gracious Queen of song, and mean to be prodigiously indifferent to her performances which will abound, I prophesy. "Spite, spite!"

Now, will you write to me once again before I go away? Goodbye, dearest friend. You have not given me certain things according to promise, the photograph [2] for one: but never mind, though I do. The boy is well, and nobody is the "world" to me in *that* sense, I should think! Other people have such a monster, however, and I fear all the more for them, from my own ignorance.

Affectionately yours,

R. B.

The Crag, Falmouth
July 29th. 1864

I am not altogether displeased with those no-accounts which sent me an order for a pin-head-

---

[1] Jenny Lind, Madame Otto Goldschmidt, (1820-1887) soprano singer. In March 1870 Browning wrote to Miss Isabella Blagden, "I have known Made Schwabe this many a day; good, impulsive, not wise at all but generous abundantly. I dined with her last year and heard Rubinstein."

[2] Presumably a photograph of Miss Wedgwood. There is a portrait of her in her book *The Personal Life of Josiah Wedgwood, The Potter*, revised and edited with an introduction and memoir by C. H. Herford; Macmillan, 1915.

drop of palm wine today, which I hasten to supply at the same time that I gratify your feminine taste in letting you have the last word on that same palm-wine subject. The palm is greatly flourishing in these genial regions—for they are very genial,—and those deep indecisions not a few, are forgotten. I am sorry you are kept in London by publishing business, for the days of July in London are not tempting, even when one has villa parties with Jenny Lind to meet. I am rather inclined to agree with you about her, though I have more respect for poor people who try to be good than you have. I hope you were not too "prodigiously indifferent," or it wd suggest epigrams to those who were clever enough. I feel as if I cd hammer one out myself if I had an ill-natured imagination, or a keener wit, but "I have not so large a mouth," as your boy said. I conceive how your anxious appreciation of the opinion of the world will awaken at such a suggestion! I wonder if we are meant to care so little for the judgment of our fellows— some of us are, I suppose, and thereby perhaps not to influence them the less.

That Sludge anecdote is a true "moral tale" to me, coupled with the other side to which you refer. I suppose one influences people mostly in that unexpected way, there yours was certainly a startlingly extreme instance. I feel as if I had slipped into an improving and sermon-like vein which will of all others be the very thing to suit your taste, so I shall work it thoroughly! I hope you will escape assassination, I am so weak and mean (as I'm afraid you'll think it) that I have a little pity for poor Mr S.—I don't mean for this last business, but for the poem, but I suppose he is the sort of man to endure being gibbetted better than most of us.

You will be glad to hear that I have cheerful letters from my mother. She writes me that she is much refreshed by a few days entire solitude, which is the best atmosphere, I think, in which to pass a certain stage of grief; it is better when all the inward lament has spoken uninterruptedly for a little. She is not a person to whom time will make much difference; not finding relief in utterance ever, it very soon becomes as hidden a thing as it ever is.

I remain here a fortnight and then return to pay some suburban visits, where the outer world will present no temptations to me and the inner world ought to produce some crop—but at the risk of hurting your feelings (for you have always implied a vast difference of age between us that makes any autumnal tinge in me mean a late December for you) I must say that I'm afraid it is too late in the day for me to do anything but improve my mind.

The "Saturday Review's" stock remark on all women's productions, "that it is gratifying to reflect that so much labour, etc. cannot but have produced valuable results to the writer, however, etc."—looms mournfully before me as the goal of all mine—unless I bring out a commentary on your works. I think I must wait till you are dead before I venture on that, and as you are so old it will not detain me long. Reading it will probably form yr occupation in Purgatory.

Ever yr. affec.

F. J. W.

Tuesday, Aug 2 '64

GOODBYE, DEAREST FRIEND.

I go tomorrow,[1] stay, as I very likely have told you, some two months, and see you prominently

---

[1] In a letter to Isabella Blagden written from 19 Warwick Crescent on the 19th of October, Browning gave a concise itinerary of his journeyings on this occasion. "I returned," he wrote, "on the 11th. We stayed three weeks at Biarritz; in the loveliest weather possible—just spent a day in Spain, to get a taste of its quality (a very pleasant one)—going to Fontarabia, Irun and St. Sebastian. We returned easily by Bayonne, Bordeaux, Tours and Paris: I only stayed one day there."

on the white cliffs as a landmark for return. We won't teaze each other with any more "last words," but take the good of understanding each other without further labour and pains: I will not be older than you like, nor you younger than I want. I daresay nothing but good will come out of it all to you and me. Remember where I shall be till I settle—151 Rue de Grenille, Faubg. St. Germ. and always inform me exactly where you are.

I have been reading your admirable article in the "Reader" [1]—admirable, I mean every letter of the word.

So, "I stretch out my hand for bread"—had you any fancy of the possible attitude in the future of
              Yours ever affectionately,
                        R. B. ?

Aug. 19, '64.   Maison Isabelline,
      Cambo, près Bayonne, Basses-Pyrénées

So far South, you see—farther than I intended: after staying at Paris a week we thought

[1] Articles in "The Reader" are not easily identified; some are initialed and many are unsigned. In the issue dated the 2nd of July 1864, there is a report of a meeting of the Philological Society when Hensleigh Wedgwood was in the chair and H. B. Wheatley read a paper "On a Family of Reduplicated Words," and on the 4th of June appeared a review of *Dramatis Personæ* occupying nearly five columns. These are not signed, but it seems not unlikely that both were written by Miss Wedgwood.

· 39 ·

of going to Arcachon, a new place by Bordeaux, but found it full of visitors and noise: three or four years ago it must have been mere sand-hill and pine-forest along the sea—now you have *boulevards* in the middle of the old trees, a casino, and the other French institutions. La Teste, nearer the city, had no houses to let, nor did I much care: so we made for Bayonne—tried St. Jean de Luz (the charming little port, with an Italian-looking frame of mountains—all to no use, every place taken: remained the formid-able Biarritz, which we looked at and left alone) —tired and teazed with travel and heat, we be-took ourselves to this pretty little village some sixteen miles from Bayonne, with the Pyrenees and woods enough: it is a mineral-spring, several indeed, that bring people here at the "season," which is not now: the Basque peasantry are somewhat interesting; anyhow, here we stay a month—till next 13th when we shall try again St. Jean de Luz: if I don't yield to my adventur-ous son who wants to go to Madrid instead—it is really but a few hours distance by railway; Spain itself, the first village in it, is eight or nine miles off. I want the sea, for myself,—though the notion of seeing the Titians and Velasquez is not a bad one.

The country is strangely green and growthful, for this time of year—the mountains like those about Florence and Siena—the little river under the village, far more abundant than you would find such a stream in Italy, comes from Navarre: in fine, there's no particular hardship in spending a month here, but it's a transparency which I have no candle to put behind: it "lights up," I daresay, to the luckier sort: besides, I am bilious and sleepy overmuch, and made little or no provision for being not impossibly bored. I have got Virgil—for the boy's plague—Euripides, for my own solace—a volume of George Sand's plays—Oh, George!—and the *Travels of Rabbi Benjamin of Tudela*,[1] which I must have been inspired to bring from Paris by an astonishing note of the translator's, evidently meant for me—you shall judge: the translator was a schoolmaster:—

"Rabbi Perida took such great care of his scholars, who from appearances were as promising as my own, that he made it a general rule to read and explain the same thing four hundred times over: but such was his fortune, that on a

---

[1] *Travels of Rabbi Benjamin, Son of Jonah of Tudela* . . . faithfully translated by the Rev. R. Gerrans, Lecturer of Saint Catherine Coleman, and Second Master of Queen Elizabeth's Free Grammar School, Saint Olave, Southwark, London, 1784.

particular occasion, one of his hopeful pupils, either through stupidity or inattention, was at the end of the lecture as wise as he was at the beginning: whereupon the Rabbi gave a specimen of his patience by repeating the same lecture over four hundred times more. At this, a voice was heard from heaven, to the following purpose, 'Perida, either live four hundred years, or obtain innocence and eternal life for thee and thy posterity!' Perida without hesitation chose the latter: but his scholars, out of cruel kindness, cried 'No, no, no—but four hundred years for Perida!'" Their request was granted: he lived four hundred years: and if he was a schoolmaster all the time, I heartily pity him.

What do you say? I keep trying to be quite intelligible, next poem: what if the "Saturday Review" should get me four hundred years more of rendering-intelligible, by general outcry to heaven? Mind, this book, printed in 1783, has my grandfather's name among the subscribers—did he foresee the lesson he was securing to his descendant? But I observed another omen at Arcachon, telling the other way, for they caught and exhibited on the beach two mighty dolphins, the biggest I ever saw—"had *le poltron* chosen to break my nets," quoth the hero of the haul, "he might have done it like a cobweb, but he thought they were strong—I know the nature of the beast and he let me get under his fin with my knife"—so the great fellow, eight feet long, was to "yield a little oil," and get *sous* from us the *badauds* as the hat went round. No, I shall charge the nets, for my part, and mind nobody's voice but   .[1] These dolphins had really heads like the old idealized creature, with respectable teeth, which I was glad to hear they knew how to use, poltrons as they were.

20th. I went this morning to see the mountain-pass called "Le pas de Roland"—the tradition being that he opened a way through a rock that effectually blocks it up, by one kick of his boot, and so let Charlemagne's army pass: it is a striking little bit of scenery, with the clear green river between the mountain-walls, not unlike the Lima at Lucca; but I think I liked best of all a great white-breasted hawk I saw sunning himself on a ledge, with his wings ready. How can you so misconceive of those *above* us, as to fear they may continue to misunderstand? Couched eyes that see none the better for that operation!—Oh, no! Then, it is so easy, wickedly easy, for people indifferent to each other

---

[1] This illegible word may be "Avison's." He was a composer.

never to quarrel: thence comes it that living in families tends to cretinize one—you find out early all about your fellows, love them always, but have no more curiosity about them, have no hope of improving them in any way, nor indeed desire it —they will *do* as they are: but you yourself will not do as you are, and if you wish another spirit to keep close by you while you go up higher, offences must come, and the wings get in the way of each other: how easily that must be seen by the bird that gets first to the height! Of course I was fortunate through the peculiarity of the relation: in that closeness there could be no misunderstanding: but had there been, I should care nothing about it now.

As for enjoying the sun,—all the enviable instants of this life seem when we push out of it into the other, to fall back again fast enough: "whether in the body or out of the body, I cannot tell": those who *can* tell that they are out of it, —do you think they envy you down among the fir-trees? But they may, in a sort, envy you the feeling you will have presently when the dark cloth is suddenly twitched from your face, and fancying yourself lost in the dark, you find yourself at home. "The world has no perdition, if some loss."—This is no chatter nor cant with me, I can tell you, but an instinct which has given worth to many formulas, before I could bear it by itself, truth and force as it is: how these formulas get true and false and then true again when unnecessary! when you can *mean* with Dante, "Thus I believe, thus I affirm, thus I am certain it is, and that from this life I shall pass to another better, there, where that Lady lives, of whom my soul was enamoured."

21st. Pray what do you mean by being such a coquette and talking about "your course, now setting toward me, which tomorrow maÿ set from me and turn no more"? Thank you,—particularly if you will instruct me as to how I should reply to such a complimentary prognostication—"Pray do so when you please—it will be quite the same to me"—or, as an itinerant corn-cutter calls after his relieved patients in Rome "I told you, you'd soon be able to run away from me!" —Or is it an ingenious way of reassuring me, in case I am compunctious at doing you possible harm? Perida, *didst* thou ever explain a thing after eight hundred times iteration? I dare say you never understood me a whit the better for my painstaking. Never mind, you will always be good enough for me. God bless you.

R. B.

This 24 of August has been made a bright day to me by the arrival of a letter from the Pyrenees. We were further apart than I thought, instead of being opposite neighbours having half Europe between us. I am sorry you have not got to the sea, which will not be substituted for by mountains and trees—that is not grammar, I am afraid, but quite good enough to go to a Poet. "Rien ne se remplace, parce que rien ne se ressemble." I like that pensée of Mme Swetchine.

How bad the best thing is, when one wants something different!—the ugly things that those transparencies are, when one's candle is extinguished. There is nothing like the vielcomfranschende Meer (do you know Voss's Iliad [1]—I am so fond of that epithet) when one has any sort of weight to throw off from body or mind. I think it is partly the entire absence of any association with man's work, one is weary sometimes at the sight of hedges and roads, thinking of the toil—but one looks at that waste of waters that refuses to retain for one moment

---

[1] Presumably Homer's *Werke* von J. H. Voss, published at Altonia in 1793.

a trace of any effort of ours, and yet makes no pause in its own, and it seems a rest to one's fancy—for I dare hardly call it one's imagination. Your Sea, by the bye, does no work of its own. I suppose I should miss the tides—the crystal rock pools with all their inhabitants, you have not them in the Mediterranean? You have mightier inhabitants, however, and I am not in doubt as to which of your omens will lead you, the dolphins or the Rabbi.

Meantime, dear friend, be assured you are always and have been always perfectly intelligible to one reader, whether through the printer's handiwork or your own, and I think that conjugation may be completed. Nay if it were not too arrogant I should add that misunderstanding was more likely, if it arose at all, to begin at the other end—from the fact of one of us being given to express every gust of thought or feeling for which wiser souls have no weathercock, and which had much better find none. There is nothing so delusive as such thinking aloud as mine. But I have no fear. I will promise you to make no outcry to Heaven that you shd live till the "Saturday" understands you as well as I do. However it (the 400 years) might

be a wholesome contingency to contemplate, for
I think you wd bear clarifying.

Here everybody is reading Tennyson. You
know I am a heretic about him—no, not a heretic, for I bow to the general creed, but only confess to a want of fervour in my response. I only
know *Enoch Arden* in your version, do you remember giving it me? You said you thought it
a fault that Enoch shd reveal himself to his wife
after his death—I think that touch of incon-
sistency makes it natural, but it wd be more
heroic to have kept the mask down. I thought
the Dedication to his wife very fragrant and
delicate [1]—Ah how weary you will be of my
boiled-down essence of post-London talk!

What a dreadful friend Mrs Cameron [2] must
be, my friends here were calling upon her during
his presence in the house, when he went out of
the room she fell upon them "Oh, now do at once
tell me what you think of his last poem" (not
this, it was some time ago). "He will be *sure* to

<hr/>

[1] A Dedication, "Dear, near and true—" in the *Enoch Arden*
volume; Moxon, 1864.
[2] Julia Margaret Cameron (1815-1879), photographer. Translated Bürger's *Leonore,* published in 1847, and wrote many poems.
She made portraits of Tennyson, Browning, Joachim and others.
Two of her portraits of Tennyson appear in the *Memoir* of his son,
who there records that "Mrs. Cameron's wildly romantic ideas and
performances used to call forth growls of amused dissatisfaction
from him, and he hated the adulatory attitude of some people." See
Browning's reply to this letter, p. 53.

ask me, but mind you do not say anything disagreeable. I always look through the newspapers to see if there is anything that wd go against him." How glad I am you have not a Mrs. Cameron! It is amusing to see how that species of woman ignores the wife. Well, there is something touching in every form of hero-worship, but from such poisoned cup-bearing, the Lord deliver us! I have seen a deal of the mischief we do in that way, upon very noble characters, I wonder which will be called to account at last—I think you, as the stronger creatures, will have the larger half to answer for. You were happy only to have the vulgar American type, pure penance. I say you were, you see; to such an aged man one anticipates that truth! I look upon your father as a sort of wandering Jew, in fact I don't believe in him. My imagination refuses to go a generation back from you. See all the veneration that is ready for you, and beware how you abuse it!

I wish I cd send you some of my books, which chiefly occupy me here. Homer is my chief friend. I wonder what the charm is of *unfeelingness* wherever it is not unnatural. One feels it in such different things, in a young animal, and in those old stories—I suppose it is a rest to our over-worked nature to find an exercise for one part of us that lets the deepest rest in a sound sleep. Of course, I don't mean there is no pathos, but it is the want of any case for humanity as such that has a sort of curious satisfaction in it.

What do you think of Max Müller [1] finding out that the siege of Troy is a mythical representation of the Dawn, Helen is the morning twilight, stolen by the Sun, and only to be restored after a long siege! Poor Helen, what hard service she has done in supporting types; I met her again in a sermon of Jeremy Taylor's where she was the one darling sin, that we would not surrender though our Troy fall for her sake. Ah, that morning twilight that is stolen from us, shall we ever find it again?—our evening twilight is something different, though it may have its own force too. How beautiful it was with the deep Heavens and the dim earth, now it is the heavens that are dim, and the earth so obtrusive.

(25th.) I wonder if you will go to Madrid, it would be a great temptation. My brother was a little disappointed in the gallery. If your boy really wants to go I am sure you will obey him. I know how absolute those monarchs are! We

---

[1] Friedrich Max Müller (1823-1900), philologist and orientalist.

have such a one in our family, the child of one who had as many months of happiness as you had years, and who is one of my greatest friends. For this reason and for no other, he is rather bound up with you in my mind. The loss is rather too recent for such speculations, but I cannot help shrinking in imagination from the time, which for a young man is natural and so I suppose right, when the absorbing grief shall yield to the mere material want of a new companion. It is so disappointing to see it, it seems to me like a sort of abdication of the rights of immortality; all my relations, who want that everybody should be *comfortable* are always anticipating it, and it always jars on me so painfully.

A barren post has just come in which disappoints me, and I turn to my yesterday's harvest again; my lean kine are very tolerable after it. Ah, if they wd only match themselves as equally as in Pharaoh's dream! [1]—but the herd are lean and the fat one is hidden among them.

I sometimes fear that the sense of immortality may be the very thing itself—that those souls which see the future have their inheritance there, but that for others, who merely live on a

---

[1] Genesis, xli.

second-hand investment of those hopes and convictions of others, as they are formulized for us in the deepest words we know, are really deluding themselves with a prospect which is not for them. In other words, that to be immortal is to know it, and then I am sure I am not. Perhaps this is the delusion of the sultry noon, when one is so tired of the journey that one could almost be content, at certain moments, to sit down by the dusty highway and fall asleep, even to wake no more. I saw my stars in the early dawn and perhaps I shall see them again in the twilight. Even at noon they may be seen from the shaft of a well, they say, and those who pass into the hidden depths of life may keep their view of the eternal through all the glaring day. But what if we get into those deep clefts and do not see them?—that also maÿ be weak eyesight perhaps.

Strange that one should understand human beings so well as I do (does that sound too arrogant?) and come upon some such strange misunderstanding with that which is in some way, expressed in all; as if I should understand your poems and not you. For the infinite that separates the man and what he makes is surely a sufficient type for the other infinite difference. "With stammering lips and an unknown tongue will I speak to this people." [1]   Others have heard that announcement, besides Isaiah.   I will not keep this, lest I shd put it into the fire.   Tell me something of your companions, young and old, and most of all of yourself and try as much as possible to banish from your very thoughts

yr ever affec.

JULIA WEDGWOOD

Cambo, près Bayonne, Basses-Pyrénées.
(till the 13th.)
Sept. 2, '64

There is all but another fortnight to pass here, and I want another letter, you understand. The place is even prettier than I thought, but I feel somehow walled-about and over-looked, as one says of London suburban houses, though the obstructions are purely spiritual in this case, the influences in the air,—for, nine times out of ten, I don't meet a soul.   But there is no sea to go out and walk on, as, I suppose, Christ used when he was sick of the world.   The sea,— "that fair scroll-finis to a wicked book"—(what perfect poetry that is!)   What is it that I have been meaning to say to you, now, in reply?

---

[1] Isaiah, xxviii, 11.   "For with stammering lips and another tongue will he speak to this people."

First, this nearest sea will not be the Mediterranean, but the Atlantic, if you please: you think I am east of the midway from Bayonne to Marseilles, whereas there are scarcely twenty miles to get back again, in case I go to St. Jean de Luz. Madrid I shall postpone, contenting the boy probably with a taste of Sebastian or Pampeluna: I want two or three weeks' bathing, and then our holiday ends.

I am not sure that I understand what you mean by "having seen stars in the early dawn" —I observe nowhere in youth, except in diseased and dying youth, the religious instincts: religious dogmas are accepted at that age undoubtingly, but they don't influence a child's actions at all—*that* business is done by quite other agents: it is curious to observe what practical atheism, so far as regards the God themselves affect to believe in, distinguishes ordinary children: they have not a natural need for what you artificially give them, and so, without at all disputing your dogmas' truth, they never apply them in any difficulty, having better ways of their own for righting matters: whereas the real instinct is developed with mature years, and, then only, substitutes itself for the previous motives which are losing their virtue of impelling or repressing one—hence the new birth: while this life suffices, I don't see that another incentive to push on through its insufficiency, in the shape of a conceived possibility of a life beyond, is ever given us. I know that I possess at this minute every advantage that I had thirty five years ago, even to the health and power of physical enjoyment—added to plenty of acquisition undreamed of at that time—and yet have outgrown all the considerations which used to manage, for better and worse, the wise person of my perfect remembrance and particular dislike—but there are now [1] finger-posts in this far end of the road, as it once seemed, and I am less than ever my own master: that, however, is far from meaning that one is clearly another's servant,—life would not be what life *is*—and is, for a good reason probably,—if one or the other relation could be clearly determined,—one could then live forever:—it is because one cannot so live on now, under the present conditions, in virtue of the very desire to live in a conceivable absolute freedom and fulness of life,—that I hope this is to be one day.

You exaggerate the horrors of Mrs. Cam-

---

[1] This word may be "new."

eron [1]—"poison," indeed!—not but she keeps a tray of brandied "lollipops," and other substitutes for honest beefsteak requisite to the natural stomach: and after all, what harm does she do Alfred? If he considered her while he made his verses, *then* indeed! As it is, there will always be a buzzing of sillinesses about such a person. Depend on it, nobody has done him the least harm at any time: nobody has more fully found out at the beginning what he was born to do,—nor done it more perfectly. He told me that when he wrote "The Gardener's Daughter" [2] he felt his life to be in flower—that he wrote "baskets-full" of similar poems at that time, emanations of the same spirit. I have not read this book yet—and know nothing of the "dedication" [3]—except that I rejoice at it, loving Mrs Tennyson singularly.

I still see that fault in Enoch Arden:—if he is to be "strong and heroic," a fault: nor a natural one, in that way, I think: Could I rule the economy of the piece, it should go thus:— after the return from the peeping in at the window, Enoch should confirm himself in his

---

[1] Mrs. Cameron, see note 2, page 48.

[2] "The Gardener's Daughter; or, The Pictures" was first published in the two-volume edition of *Poems*, Moxon, 1842.

[3] See note 1, page 48.

resolution "never to let her know," and only admit those other fancies of her learning the truth after his death, and of his children seeing their father once again,—as impossible luxuries, to be put down *as* fancies, because destructive, if carried into fact, to what is the only purpose of his life now: and so fancying, and so repressing fancies, he should quietly die in his hole. And then on a mellow autumn evening, the right time for a nutting excursion, should the happy family from the mill sally forth, with a tender reminiscence of old days, toward the well-known brow of the hill, and the hollow where the bushes abound, and there come upon a pauper's funeral, the cart and the four rough planks—and be so set, the party, upon natural speculations. The young man, with the sagacity of his age, should divine that the poor devil could be no other than that odd, disreputable-looking and suspicious character who used to skulk about the ale-house, as if he had reasons enough for avoiding the constable, and—telling on his fingers—wonder whether it could be Giles the Poacher, or Jack the Gypsey [*sic*] that had to do with the setting the barn on fire,—or peradventure George the Tinker that decamped from his wife and children, leaving them a present to the parish? Thereupon should the Miller, whose thumb is proverbially made of gold,—he should "improve" the occasion by inculcating on the young ones the evil consequences of self-indulgence,—how man is made to conquer his riotous desires, not yield to them "like this publican," while the Mother, the faithful Annie, though setting a proper example by turning up the white of her eyes, should treat herself to a little retrospective thankfulness— acknowledging that after a little roughness things had come satisfactorily round, and that, worst coming to the worst, dear Enoch's brave death in the storm,—was it not better for him, and these beloved ones, than that he should . . . who can tell? . . . have lived on, even for such an end as this! And so they should proceed to their nutting, and Enoch, by a series of jolts, to his harbour in the churchyard—and we, to the considerations appropriate to one more view of this world.

And now, goodbye till I have taken a stroll— after I have added, though, that the concluding touch in the poem about the fine funeral,— which Tennyson gave me to understand was a very pregnant one,—strikes me as ambiguous and unlucky—it coincides too exactly with an impudent speech in an old French play, I remember, wherein a gallant thus addresses his mistress, "And, talking of brutebeasts, how does your husband do? Whenever is he intending to die, that fellow? Let him make haste, and I promise him the finest of funerals!" [1]

By the bye, there is another thing which I want to say, in explanation of something I wrote —about one's family not "growing," proportionately to one's own growth. I meant *symmetrically*, rather: for they may grow just as you grow, only—here's the fault—you none of you profit by each others' growth, it is not in your direction, but for somebody else to profit by—much as with a cluster of fruits on a common twig: each may bulge out round and red enough in the sun's eye, but the place where all the clustered knobs touch, where each continues to be known to the other, *that* is as hard and green, and insipid as ever, and if peach can only judge of fellow-peach by that place of junction and communion, the result's generally poor enough. Or *is* it generally so? I am inclined to go into extremes, and want, as you say "we poets do," intensity at price of all other qualities. And now for the wood.

---

[1] The closing lines of *Enoch Arden* read:—"And when they buried him the little port had seldon seen a costlier funeral."

Sept. 3. Yes, the seed of beauty that "Helen" has scattered all over the world is infinite: I don't know many memorable paintings nor statues [1] of her—but in music, I have been remembering these thirty years & more Glück's overture to "Helen and Paris," [2] and wondering whether the rest of the work could keep up to the tone of that—exactly what you remark in Homer—that far-away carelessness of common hopes and fears: I was speaking of it, *so*, to Hallé [3] not two months ago, and playing it to him on the table-cloth. In my last good days at Rome, the best in my life, I was meaning to do what I could "next year," with a subject that struck me—Helen dedicating a goblet, which reproduced the perfection of what Virgil calls "exsertae mammae", and was deposited in the temple of Venus,—a group of her, bidding farewell to the imperishable beauty, and a young priest receiving the same, and revolving other comparisons: on mentioning this to my friend Rossetti, [4] "I'll paint it" said he—and there it is, archaically treated indeed. Then, what a

---

[1] This word may be "studies."

[2] C. W. Glück (1714-1787). His "Paride ed Elena" was produced in Vienna in 1770.

[3] Sir Charles Hallé (1819-1895), pianist and conductor. He was a native of Westphalia.

[4] Gabriel Charles Dante Rossetti (1828-1882).

strange fancy is that of Euripides on which he has founded his whole play of *Helena*—"that it was not really Helen, only an apparition of her, that fled to Troy, and caused all the fighting,— the true Helen living sadly and saintly in Egypt, having been stolen by Mercury at the command of Juno and confided to the care of Proteus the King,—at whose tomb her husband finds her again, wringing her hands at the world's misconception of her character through the doings of the *eidolon*. Qy: does this mean, a good poem suffering from the world's misconception of it? There,—take your revenge on my *eidolon* for this string of rags and tatters, and be sure that (in Egypt) I am,

ever affectionately yours,

R. B.

Combe Hurst, Kingston-on-Thames, London, S.W.

for another fortnight.

Friday, Sept. 9th, 1864
Combe Hurst

I think I must begin my letter if it is to travel all across France before the 13th. I hope you will find a bit of sea to get to by that time—who

calls the sea "scroll-finis to a wicked world?"—
that is a very modern booky metaphor, but
fixes itself in one's mind as something appropriate. Poetry is all ready-made in the sea, the
most commonplace real thoughts about it are
poetic, any mind that gives back a mere echo of
what is there is poetic for the time; and vice
versa, it seems to me poets can write very pro-
saically about it, to judge from Tennyson's
"Sea Dreams." [1]

I was much amused with your hypothetical
funeral for Enoch, but it is only saying there is
material in the facts for a different set of ideas,
you could not introduce that bit of Rembrandt
shadow anywhere in the little water colour
sketch as it is without spoiling it. I don't think
he could deal effectively with that irony of fate,
it would not fit in with his style of execution,
and it seems to me the very exception you take
to the grand funeral is a proof of it, for what is
intended is just this allusion, I suppose, and instead of being forcible it is unsatisfactory, like
a sudden modulation in his last bar.

The only thing I enjoy in the book is the
Lincolnshire farmer, which is to me delicious.

---

[1] "Sea Dreams," first published in *Macmillan's Magazine*,
January 1860, was included in the *Enoch Arden* volume.

Like E. W. I believe it was an expansion of a fact, one of the verses I heard quoted, at least, as a real speech before the book came out. I think the perfect paganism of the man's feeling, and the devout absorbedness in "The land"—the grand indifference to his own prospects in comparison—favor the most emphatically a work of *genius* of anything he has ever done, for it is most of a creation. I write on the supposition that he read you that with the others: unless he had a very different comparative estimate of the value of those poems, he must have done so.

I liked his Dedication less on a 2nd reading, there is a little too much about himself in it and not enough about his wife. I wish I could get into a right spirit of appreciation of him. I know so many little unpleasantnesses of him, and though that is not a good standpoint to take with reference to a great poet, one can't help being influenced by it. Rather like judging the tree by the caterpillars that drop off it, you will say. In this Dedication, for instance, I can't help seeing an unhealthy liveliness of perception of his critics, and there is one little poem about his own poetry [1] that put me into a rage.

---

[1] "The Flower"; see note 1, page 98.

Talking of appreciation, I have been so much interested in the few reminiscences which Hilary Bonham Carter (I think you know her) was giving me of your wife, as it struck me that there was a singular degree of appreciation of her, for the slight degree of their intercourse. I have hardly ever seen any one else who knew her, so there was perhaps an adventitious interest in her recollections to me. I was looking into *Aurora Leigh* for something that expressed what I meant about the dawn. "Observe, *I* mean in youth,— just *I* the conscious and eternal soul, etc." I will never say anything so foolish as "do you remember?" any passage of hers.—Ah, really I don't think there is anything very valuable in those vistas that seem to open on every side into the infinite in the early days, they are mere pictures that we take for windows, and some of them perhaps hang before and hide the real windows, but one regrets the infinite possibilities of youth, unreal as they are. I was not thinking of children's experience when I spoke of it. I always went to bed as a child elaborately expecting the Judgment Day; remembering that passage about its coming as a thief in the night, and not feeling sure about my own account in the reckoning, I thought that the best measure to keep it off.

If I held the same opinion now as to the influence of my large expectations on that small matter, they might be arranged differently. That kind of anticipation is an unfortunate enough element in a child's life, and it is the natural form which is taken in a child's mind by what are true grown-up motives and beliefs—so far I agree with you in what you say of their practical atheism.

Yes, I am afraid I agree with you in the peach-cluster theory, but when one sees a peach which has succeeded in elongating its own stalk sufficiently to detach itself from that parent cluster one feels that it is not unmixed advantage. Miss Bonham C., for instance, though she is a highly favoured specimen. Art has been to her the gold of the fable, she has dug her vineyard to some purpose and has produced a goodly crop of friends, but I think the Art is nought. We have been all inspecting her statuette of Florence Nightingale, [1] which has occupied four good years of her life, and is—well, I don't think I shd have been much less unwilling to have spent

---

[1] Miss Bonham Carter modelled the statuette under the supervision of Thomas Woolner, R. A. (1825-1892), whose marriage to Miss Alice Gertrude Waugh took place on the 6th of September, 1864. Miss Carter died the following year and Woolner wrote of her to Mrs. Tennyson, "there never was a finer creature in intelligence and active goodness."

4 years over a beautiful piece of embroidery. How melancholy it is to think of all the large amount of life and thought and emotion that may be put into a work of any kind, and be completely absorbed by it, leaving no trace to any eye but the originator. I thought of the 2 women that were employed on the little doll as subject and object, and marvelled at the poverty of the result.

F. N., too, is one of those detached peaches— better so on the whole, doubtless, better for the sake of the world as herself—but meantime not without heavy loss. We have been all much interested in her Woolner's marriage, [1] which took place on Tuesday. He is a sort of adopted younger brother of Miss Carter's, who went to the wedding and described the pretty bride to us—quite dainty enough to marry a sculptor, to judge from her photograph,—an exception to the general run of photos, as they were cleverly described by one of the Lushingtons, as having for their chief value "to be worn next the heart in cases of unrequited attachment." This particular one was only fitted to aggravate the complaint. I hear W. is a great habitué of Mr

---

[1] See note 1, page 65.

Carlyle's, I daresay he will stand that atmosphere better than poor Ruskin.

I thought I might have been nearer you by the width of the Channel by this time, as my elders are gone to a German bath, and I offered to go and take care of them, but my services were declined with ardour—perhaps founded on no inadequate conception of my capacities as courier. I am well satisfied not to exercise them for my own part. That Euripidean Helen is what Plato works so hard in the Republic—another type for the poor overworked lady! Ah no, the Eidolon theory has a broader application than to poems or poets, which if they are really good suffer mighty little from the world's want of appreciation; it is for more common-place mortals that wait wringing their hands in Egypt, while the Eidolon plays unseemly pranks in Troy. I wish you wd take that subject that you meditated, it is one of the most capacious conceivable.

Farewell, dear friend [1]

---

[1] Miss Wedgwood did not always sign her letters.

Maison Gastonbide, Plage des Basques,
Biarritz, Basses-Pryénées.

Sept. 19 '64

Do you see what a scrap of writing this cannot otherwise than be?   The meaning of the
piece of a sheet is, that I was frightened this
morning by a calculation made betwixt asleep
and awake as to the possibilities of hearing from
you before I leave this place, which must happen
on the 30th, and may happen on the 28th—so
I shall say my word, and (parenthetically) see
what you are made of, trying your generosity,
as a friend should sometimes—for I shall count
the lines of the reply to this and determine
whether you give me one the less: it is in the
proprieties of our friendship that I should ask
favours occasionally.   Once when I was at
Rome there befell me some chance of being
presented to the Pope—(Gregory, that was)—
and on my landlord, an old Roman, hearing of
it, said he, "What favour shall you ask him?"
—"Why, what should I ask?"—"Oh, it's im-
proper to ask nothing—as if you were in no need
of him, indeed!"—However, I did not go, did
not ask, and only put this pretty lesson to use

this same early morning at Biarritz—where I find myself stationed by sheer inability to move elsewhere—St. Jean de Luz, whereto I was inclined, being still filled with Spaniards glad to use the new railway.

This house is close to the sea, and out of the heart of the noisy town, and we do well enough for the little while that is to be cared for. The sea-view, with the mountains, make all amends: there are extraordinary tides, too, and the standing attraction at one of the bathing-places is the increasing probability of somebody's being drowned in a certain ugly current which sucks you unawares under the rock: I saw one man who, two days ago, all but gave us the due entertainment. Now, then—what were we talking about?

I know Miss B. Carter, and like her much,—though she don't believe it, on account of a failure on my part of going to some party to which she invited me. I ought to have seen that statuette—and now do see it, exactly, through your eyes, and, Simeon-like, may depart in peace. Confess that *my* subject argues the more artistic nature—(*mine* because I found it, of course, did not invent it.) As to the poem about the old Farmer, [1] I am certain, from the remarks on it of the two or three people who have written to me, that I shall enjoy it enormously: all I know of the book is "Enoch Arden"—and the old pieces, of course.

There, my letter is wanted—now, I shall see what I shall see!—if I see a letter of yours before I leave.

Ever your affectionately,
R. B.

Thursday, Sept. 22nd, '64
Combe Hurst

Not much fear of my letter not hitting you, you see. I am well accustomed to "false quantity" from all my correspondents, as everybody knows what a gift of the gab I have on paper and that there is no danger of my stopping too soon when I begin to write. You do not say where you are going to after Biarritz—which sounds a horribly commonplace and fashionable retreat for you. I suppose you are among the bathers, so that you have the excitement of being

---

[1] On the 13th of October, 1864, Browning wrote to Tennyson from Warwick Crescent, "I have been two months away, and only just found your book now. . . . Enoch continues the perfect thing I thought it at first reading, but the Farmer, taking me unawares, astonished me more in this stage of acquaintanceship."

nearly drowned yourself, as well as the entertainment of watching it in others.

I think if I write a long letter in answer to yours, a rule-of-three sum wd exhibit a wonderful debtor and creditor account between us, considering the proportion of my material to my production, and comparing it with yours. I have not left this villa nor seen but one face, since you went to Cambo. Nevertheless, it is odd that I don't find few things to say to you.

I quite long for you to see the "Northern Farmer," it is so charming. Oh what a horrible young lady epithet!—It reminds me of a friend of mine who took another friend to Mr. Hunt's [1] studio to see that moonlight picture. "Oh, very nice—but what is that blue thing in the sky?" I was amused at the idea of Hunt having a young lady to tell him his picture was nice, and having to explain to her that an object in the sky was the moon.

To go back to my old Lincolnshire pagan—I think it must be, so to speak, a sort of accident that it is so vigorous. I mean that I don't think the kind of merit it has is in the author, but must be contained in an aspect of character familiar to him in early life which is rather a photograph

---

[1] William Holman Hunt, 1827-1910.

in his memory than a picture in his imagination. Just as one comes upon real poetry sometimes in the utterance of those who have nothing poetic in them. Or am I too Athenian-like to our Aristides? I hope there will be another poem for my perverted taste when I see you again. You know you promised me an early instalment of it; if you will reward me with that I will try to appreciate poor Enoch a little better. But I am afraid Biarritz can't be very propitious. Who knows but I may save you from the fate of your Rabbi schoolmaster!—Or do you not tremble still more at this commentary I am going to publish the moment you are dead? But no, I fancy we may say what we like about you then, and even less than now you will care.

I came upon a sentence in Plato that reminded me of something you said in a letter. "Dost thou not think that some of the departed would return to us, if Hades retained them by any weaker bond than that of desire?" And of course the docile pupil agrees with him. It is a grand utterance of the infancy of the world when desire had not tried its wings long enough to beat against the bars of a cage that is wide enough to be sometimes forgotten. I am afraid now we should not feel that unhesitating con-

viction that desire *is* the strongest of bonds. Yet
there is something of grandeur in Heathen con-
tempt for death that we can never attain to.
And then I fancy there was a Spring freshness in
the atmosphere of this poor little Earth, that we
have lost. "We look before and after and sigh
for what is not." [1] Don't you think Plato would
have been horribly disappointed to have looked
forward 2000 years and seen—us? Our little
Sun is much better furnished, no doubt, but the
sojourn seems long.

All the Reviews are busy with Newman's
Apologia.[2] They all fall foul of him for that in
him which I admire, his courageous denial of
all sleek optimist theories. Truly it seems a
wondrous leap from the conviction that *those*
are false to the Church of Rome, but in the
early divergence between him and his critics I
side with the poor priest. There is something
wonderfully typical in the passage of arms between the Apostle of the flesh and the last of the
Ascetics. Can you not fancy some future
Strauss sublimating it (is there such a word?)
into an allegorical representation of the tenden-
cies of the age. "The dominant spirit of that

[1] Shelley, "To a Skylark," stanza 18.
[2] See note 1, page 12.

material, positive, luxurious age extorts by its arrogance a feeble protest from the keen and narrow enthusiasm of an expiring asceticism. The secular virtues of a hard worldly character are brought out in rigid relief against that dying mysticism." Poor Newman! there is something very pathetic to me in the aspect of his painful unveiling before the world that is so soon to shrivel in Hell fire. One sees both inconsistent feelings are so intense. I don't know on the whole that I have less sympathy with that ardent sense of Hell, than with what I may call the spirit of the "Saturday Review." Leave out that part of it which nobody really imagines or believes, and the conviction of unsounded depths below us seems to me not only truer, but a better guide in life than that general comfortable feeling that after all there's not so much difference between one course of action and another, or one character and another—there are compensations everywhere, some people suffer more, but then their sense of enjoyment is keener, etc., etc.

Do you remember a discussion we had about the patient Grizzel (*sic*), the nut-brown maid, etc.? I was reminded of it by a very graceful little German version of *Griselda,* a tragedy of a man named Kalm, where the moral of the story is exactly inverted. Griselda bears all her husband's treatment with meek faith, but when he comes to take her back and tell her he has only been tormenting her, she bursts out into indignant refusal to have anything more to do with him, very refreshing to one's feelings, and in spite of his passionate repentance, goes back alone to her father's hut. I like any protest against the woman's tendency to servility, for all poems and fiction are so fond of the opposite view.

Now I think I deserve a full measure pressed down and running over to be returned unto me! That abundant requital may come to me at Lady Inglis, Milton Bryan, Wodburn, Beds. where I shall spend the 1st 10 days of October, after which I am to be seen at C. P.[1] and my company is particularly edifying about 1 o'clock on Sundays!

Farewell, dear friend

151 Rue de Grenille,
Faubourg St. Germain, Paris.
Biarritz, Oct. 3 '64

Still here, you see, and till the 7th, Friday, on which morning we leave for Bordeaux, Tours,

---

[1] Cumberland Place.

and Paris—three days' easy travelling—and then, after another week at most, London—say on the 15th or 16th—a Sunday, by my calculation: but if . . . where do I catch this mean spirit? . . . if you let me have a letter at Paris to re-assure me that you will be found again at Cumberland Place, I will write and tell you for certain. I shall be glad to see you, do you know?

We stayed a little beyond the appointed time in order to get more of the wonderful weather and warm, wide sea: the heat is only too Southern, none of us are "braced," as by the Breton rough procedure, but slackened rather. The bright noisy people keep on their own side of the little town, and my son likes brightness and noise, if I do not. The blue mountains of Spain are a stone's throw off. This day week we crossed the little boundary-river and landed at Fontarabia—a delicious little ruined old city, with such silent houses, and curved eaves, and wrought-balconies—I could live with the three or four dozen inhabitants, and die there, "Where Charlemagne with all his peerage fell," [1] comfortably alone, as my dear old Landor [2] has just

---

[1] Milton, *Paradise Lost*, Book I, 1:586.
[2] Walter Savage Landor, b. 1775; he died at Florence on the 17th of September, 1864.

accomplished that feat,—"without pain, and, at the last, very patient."

We then lounged for hours at Irun, close by, —my best sight and instruction being from the Spanish management of a fan by a Christian sister with whom, preferably to Miss Wedgwood, Father Newman may expect to go shares in the next world: I did not quite follow the accompaniment, but I think I am right in saying that "Et Incarnatus Est" is properly exemplified by suddenly letting drop the whole rainbow of the outward rim, suspending it in midway fall by a little-finger artfully projected, then changing sides, and somehow bringing the right extremity to the left, so that you had half a group of Watteau shepherdesses and swains and half a tessellated pavement, or what looked like it— "et-factus-est"—*snap!* and the lady grasped a solid black truncheon, pointed at the nose of the unbeliever. I should like to write an answer to the *Apologia* in fan-language: I am afraid that the appropriate illustration of "Where their worm dieth not" was detected by me in a certain vigorous application of the handle-end to that amazing knob of "back-hair" which was hidden by the lace-veil. Well, we went to St.

Sebastian, and tasted further the Spanish quality, which I am inclined to like much.

Yes, poor Landor is off and away at last—I wish him well with all my heart: he wrote to me a month ago,—"probably about to die in a few weeks or days," but he had cried "Wolf!" so often. Five years care about him, and now he is past me. He has written passages not exceeded in beauty and subtlety by any literature that I am acquainted with; that is my opinion, other people have theirs; he was followed to the grave by two of his sons, and nobody else—the grand old solitary man, beset by weaknesses just as, in his own words, "the elephant is devoured by ants in his inaccessible solitudes." Bless us, if he had let the world tame him and strap a tower on his broad back, what havoc he would have made in the enemy's ranks!—as it was, they let off squibbs at him and he got into a rage and ran off, topsey-turveying his friends right and left. I'll tell you how he talked—the rather that I might not be impudent enough to tell you, if it occurred to me on next edifying Sunday morning's colloquy. "Mrs Landor called to-day" said I. "Ha—why, you did not let her in —never surely let *her* in?"—"Oh, I should let a dog in, even, bearing your name on the collar!"—"Oh, ay, a *dog*—good! but a——?"

Methinks I have a pleasure in remembering that he "gave her her own," now that the dead lion is being appraised as "worth" so much to the living Landors.

My friend, am I intelligible? Write and hold out a light, if I am ever to swim across the dark strait from Boulogne to the Abydos of Warwick Crescent, which invites me very little otherwise. *Orsu!*

> Onward, my merry men,
> Just [1] a stroke more,—and then,

Poor L. ended! Is that mine or whose? that I hum it ever and anon? I have got the whole of that poem,[2] you enquire about, well in my head, shall write the Twelve books of it in six months, and then take breath again.

Ever yours affectionately,
R. B.

---

[1] This word may be "first."
[2] *The Ring and the Book.* Volumes I and II were published by Smith, Elder and Company in 1868, volumes III and IV in 1869.

After Oct 17th at A. J. Scott [1] Esq.,
Halliwell Lane,
Cheetham Hill, Manchester

Tuesday, October 10th. 1864
Milton Bryan

Many thanks, dear friend, for your specimen
of Fan-language, which presented me with a new
and interesting phase of the *Apologia* contro-
versy. But I don't give my consent to any
hieroglyphics on the subject! You must treat us
respectfully and not fling us torn scraps of meaning, leaving us to supply the gaps (which however I can always do)—as was suggested at the
time of the Civil Service examination contro-
versy, if I remember rightly, by way of testing
the shrewdness and imagination of the candi-
dates, and it did not seem to me such a bad idea.
Don't give us any more Palimpsests *without* the
chemical test; that makes all the difference. But
I'm afraid you are in too great a hurry to get
away from us to take any pains about our opinion
of you being a correct one. Wait a few weeks,
till I come to London and bid you goodbye, (for
I am not, after all, returning home just yet).
Ah no, you wd not wait an hour if you could

---

[1] Alexander John Scott, (1805-1866), divine; first principal of
Owens College, Manchester.

help it, and yet you don't know what Purgatory may be in store for you; you may be shut up with Saturday reviewers, or Methodist preachers, for all you know to the contrary—I wonder which you wd like the best.

Poor old Landor! [1] and so he has gone to that land in which he had not much interest! There is something grand in that carelessness for one's own experiences, in any form, but the Pagan nature perplexes one. I hope after *his* purgatory he will be admitted to the ashphodel meadows, with Pericles and his other friends, to whom I shd think he had afforded much entertainment if they have any means of getting at our poor utterances. It must be a strange sort of interest to see a virtual contemporary having lost his way on the stream of Time, and committed the anachronism of coming into the world 2000 years too late, and I shd think his friends wd give him a hearty welcome after his long wandering. Well, I suppose he went through this world without whining and moaning, and I have a kind of respect (with whatever reserves) for anybody who does that for 90 years—even at the best of things, much more with an ungrateful wife and children. We are all so miserably weak!

[1] See note, 1, page 76.

And so you are to find your little Florence grown into a grand lady when you pay her your next visit. No, I think you will not pay her a visit till her day of grandeur has come and gone. It seems to me like a gleam of sunshine passing over that memorial tablet that my sisters described to me—or torchlight rather than sunlight perhaps—some passing light that falls on a particular spot and brings out whatever one most looks to see there. I am glad you did not go there this year—it is too soon and too late. Oh, how places can hurt one! But I hope, or rather know, that you are corned against the worst hurts.

I shall not be in town next Sunday or for several Sundays, but if you are in our regions you will go and see my mother, won't you?, who will feel pleasure at seeing you in the midst of that dreary return to a life that is emptied of everything almost. Ah, dear friend, how I hope you may not survive your son; is he strong and healthy? And yet I daresay it wd not be so terrible to you, remembering whom he wd join —otherwise the grief of a parent is almost too hard!—I am going to pay a visit to another great friend of mine, who is also an aged man!, a race in which I chiefly take delight. His wife I like too, but she is too adoring and too Cameronian, and has spoilt her husband. I daresay I shall have a line from you with the address which I give accordingly.

I am spending such a tranquil visit here with two old ladies and two cats; our time chiefly spent in prayers and meals and the day is half gone before one can do anything else. We have a bit of youth to contemplate in the kitten, but I almost supply that to these ladies. I feel as if the sleepy Dutch atmosphere must infect my letter, but as I consider you rather unappreciative of the sleepy Dutch element in life it will not be the worse reading for you on that account, if you ever get through it. To be sure, I have no means of enforcing *that* result and had accordingly better not make it too long.

Do you see anybody in Paris? I hear Lord Houghton [1] is somewhere in France, hearing his footman say French verbs every morning, he writes to his children and finds him a better pupil than them. I thing that trait is pleasantly characteristic of him. I saw such a rapturous honeymoon letter from Mr Woolner—or did I write you of that? Miss B. C. [2] does not find

[1] Richard Monckton Milnes, first Baron Houghton (1809-1885), author and statesman.

[2] See note 1, page 65.

everybody of my opinion about her statuette. I am glad to see she has been asked for it for a vignette for a book of philanthropy. Now dear friend I will release you. Mind and not to be near C. P. without going in.

Ever affly yrs.,

F. J. WEDGWOOD

Friday, Octr. 14th. 64

Milton Bryan

I daresay you will have received my Paris letter, telling you that I am not to be at home for some weeks and asking you next Sunday, or when you are in that region, to pay my mother a visit instead of me. She will be so glad to see you. I am glad to think of you at home again— *home* is a word, however, which you will hardly accept as being relevant here, I fear, or for the rest of your pilgrimage. I can so well imagine how each return seems more purposeless than the last. Oh, how long life is!

I am here till Friday 21st. Whether I care for your letters I believe you know pretty well, but I daresay you will be busier now you are returned to London and I hardly expect to have them often. Farewell, dear friend

Oct. 17, '64

I shall always have time for you, time enough to say one or two words which shall be good as so many hundreds—and that, or any quantity of written matter you should have too, if it were not that the nearness puts out my voice as much as sunshine does a fire: when no sun is obtainable, I think of the coals. One or two words will be enough from me to you—not from you to me, however—because and because!

I called yesterday and spent a delightful half hour with your Mother. Let it mortify your proud-flesh, if you have any,—I did not, and shall not go to see her because you tell me to do so, but from a real pleasure it gives me—It would seem intrusive if I repeated my visit next Sunday, or I should do so: I leave the proprieties under your direction now and always, but, inasmuch as I would please you if I could by calling on almost anybody (Don't throw your glove into Mr Hume's den,[1] though!)—it is but fair to say that *this* does not count for a *corvée*.

---

[1] Possibly a reference to D. D. Home, or Hume, see note 1, page 34.

My boy,[1] whom you enquire about, is a healthy, big fellow for his fifteen years—and there's no salvation in it as assurance against a fever or a sore-throat: I am pale, and used to be thin, and never had a serious illness in my life: two bad sore-throats I remember—my mother nursed me in the first, and I wrote "Paracelsus"[2] as soon as I recovered; I remember I was a little lightheaded one long night, and fancied I had to go through a complete version of the Psalms by Donne, Psalm by Psalm! Fact! Yes, I had another slight touch of something unpleasant in the head which came on, one Good *Saturday,* as I sat reading the revise of "Pippa Passes"[3]—and my hair was cut off, but I soon got well: I wrote in bed such a quantity of that "Hippolytus," of which I wrote down the prologue, but forgot the rest, though the resuscitation-scene which was to have followed, would have improved matters: I also conceived the whole of "The Blot in the Scutcheon" and put it down easily in five days; then I had a worse than ever sore-throat and was

---

[1] Pen Browning; see note 1, page 2.

[2] *Paracelsus,* published by Effingham Wilson in 1835.

[3] "Pippa Passes," No. 1 of *Bells and Pomegranates,* published by Moxon in 1841; "Hippolytus," in "Artemis Prologizes," in Dramatic Lyrics, *Bells and Pomegranates,* No. 111, 1842; "A Blot on the Scutcheon" was No. V, 1843.

cured by Father Prout [1] forcing himself into my bedroom and making me drink hot spiced wine, —my servant Alessandro protesting "Questo pretaccio vuol ammazzare il Signore!—" I could not get sleep for the pain, and my wife took my head in her two little hands, in broad daylight, and I went to sleep at once, and woke better, and next morning, an imposthume [2] bout, but not much of a thing but enough, and I was well—and that's sixteen years ago and more. Yet I have just heard that Trollope [3] was so struck by my altered looks last year that he warned George Barrett of what was soon to come, who wrote to his sister Arabel to enquire, who replied that she didn't notice anything particular.

And here am I spared to read the "Edinburg" [4] this morning. The clever creature rummages over my wardrobe of thirty years' accumulation, strips every old coat of its queer button or odd tag and tassel, then holds them out, "So Mr. B. goes dressed now!"—of the cut of the coats, not a word. I had fancied that the bug-

---

[1] Father Prout—the Rev. Francis Sylvester Mahoney (1804-1866), humorist and journalist.
[2] This word is doubtful.
[3] Thomas Adolphus Trollope (1810-1892), author.
[4] Browning's *Poems* in three volumes, 1863, and *Dramatis Personæ*, 1864, were reviewed in the "Edinburgh Review," October 1864, pp. 537-565.

holes of that crazy old bedstead were plugged-up at this time of the day,—but no, here is the nastiness on one again! or rather off already, for to smash it would make things worse. See how I enlarge my boundaries—the two words I meant to write, the two hundred I have written! Keep well and come back soon! I dined where I met Houghton on Friday: I was put out of patience by him lately, but all is right again for the quarter of an hour: and next time, I shall remember he is a friend of yours.

God bless you,

R. B.

Hailliwell Lane, Cheetham Hill, Manchester. (A. J. Scott Esq.) Oct. 21, 1864

I was very glad to have a double account of yr visit on Sunday, whereby I can give it a stereoscope-like solidity to my mind's eye. My mother was greatly pleased to hear so much of Italian politics as she says you told her, it being a subject especially near her heart, but she is a worshipper of Mazzini,[1] which is perhaps what has set her perverse children on the other tack. I

[1] Joseph Mazzini (1805-1866), Italian patriot.

have had to help in getting up Bazaars for him, so I have a right to hate him, but I won't speak of him as you do of your reviewers, you arrogant personage! Do remember what a very dull thing justice is. How is the poor reviewer to put any smart writing into anything so laborious as a faithful estimate of another mind—whereas, if he may best light up his own little caricature we all think him so mighty clever! For my part, the books I love best almost seem to me to have their oddities, which however I look upon *not* as odd "tags and tassels" but as the prickly stems of the furze bush, which must not be rooted up by anybody who cares for those "mountain gorses ever golden—cankered not the whole year long" [1] which have done for me something of what she assigns to the flower—but if a man chooses to paint my dear furze bush at some rare season when not a blossom is to be seen, I account him neither botanist nor artist, but shall I therefore trample him under my feet, my dear brethren? You see I am making out my right to receive visitors on Sunday afternoons!

Lord Houghton has plenty of claims on your

---

[1] Mountain gorses ever golden
    Canker'd not the whole year long.
       (Mrs. Browning's "Lessons from the Gorse," stanza I, lines 1-2.)

tolerance and can afford to lose the false   [1] of being a friend of mine. I never spoke to him in my life that I remember, but he has done one deed that rather pleased me! I wonder how the poor man put you out of patience and how large the stock was that was suddenly exhausted. I wish I could fit you out with a large store of that commodity, which I think likely to be much wanted in the next few years if foolish gossip proves much of a drain on it. In a year or two it will wither away—the gossip, I mean, not the patience; which I hope will flourish all the more for exercise; perhaps I may contribute to the good work of supplying that. I must take care where I throw my glove, as you are self-bound not to fling it into my face on your escape.

I have heard others express the same opinion as Mr Trollope's [2] on your altered looks, at least, as to the fact, not with the same dismal inference, but I daresay you don't think it dismal. I sometimes wonder that all conventional expression has arranged itself on the theory that one is glad to stay as long as possible in this world. But those hands that hold the aching head are strong links here, till they become strong and painfully

---

[1] Word not clear; probably "one."
[2] See page 87.

stretched links in another direction, but even so I hope that invisible touch is felt by you still— for surely a fuller life only opens to a fuller exercise of that power, which is so shackled here at its best, and yet is the only joy in this world.

Have you seen Miss Cobbe's *Italics*? [1] and are they worthy of being seen, in spite of the affected title? I suppose she knows something of the subject, but I think you said she was not a knowing party. I shall be here about a fortnight. I am glad of your rare illnesses—illness is no great evil if the right person is there, but when that is all in the past it would be a grievous trial. It consoles me much to remember my brother's words to me in his last illness, that he was thankful to think it was unlikely he should survive our mother. Your consolation is the inversion of his, but in each case the survivor was best able to endure, I trust. Forgive me that my own thoughts lead me so much to your sacred place. I know that you are always there—but one likes to be there alone.

Ever yr affec.

F. J. W.

[1] Frances Power Cobbe (1822-1904), philanthropist and religious writer: the book referred to is, *Italics: Notes on Italy in 1864*.

Am I really to see you next Sunday? No, I
fancy. This is only going to be a word, however,
just as if I were certain of the better thing. I
ought to have written at once, having an impulse
to do so, but there were many calls on my time
and I waited too long. I am not going to let
another day go by, however, without speaking
after being spoken to,—and saying *this* particularly that you never are in my way in the "sacred
place" you speak of, and, so far as you go, I like
walking with you. Nobody else goes many
inches over the threshold of it.

Yes, I took up that book of Miss Cobbe's, at
the Athenaeum on Saturday—and found a
part in which I was concerned: well-meant, poor,
inexact, painful and mistaken stuff, all of the
performance, I should judge, from the samples
I came upon. The first fact in the portion about
us was—that Azeglio,[1] to Miss Cobbe's wonder,
had never even heard of my wife's name: for all
that, he called on her, on the strength of his
ignorance perhaps, and told me it was only
proper in him so to do. I suspect Miss C. can-

[1] Marchese d'Azeglio (1798-1866), Italian patriot and statesman;
Browning met him in Rome in the spring of 1859.

not understand, nor express herself, in Italian. All the other people she went on to describe were well known to me,—and "done" as well.

So, I am arrogant for not taking this step on the stool of humility—pronouncing, to-wit, that a mean piece of work which (it is easily said) would be impossible to me as pocket-picking, may yet be the proper and pardonable occupation of "my brethren": eh, my friend and fellow-student, will you, please, to oblige me and get fifty pounds, review Tennyson, giving extracts from his *Poems by Two Brothers,* as fitly representing what he now produces, and, including the new book in the title of your critique, give a line or two from "The Ringlet," say of "The Farmer," that is "irreverent," and so—end? Do you answer, "*I* do this?—No,—but if Miss Eldrid should diversify her life by doing so, my heart would yearn over her!" I know I cannot bring myself to think that dishonesty should be harder to my man here than to me: if it *is,* good-bye to him, and my anger for time and, I do hope, eternity! You don't, of course, confound one's classing a creeper definitely as *Cimex Edenburgensis* (graveolens Reevii)[1]—for mere

---

[1] Henry Reeve (1813-1895), man of letters; editor of the "Edinburgh Review" from 1855 to 1895. Browning surely must have been very annoyed to permit himself to apply so objectionable an epithet to Reeve.

science's sake,—with being put out of temper by the thing: there happens to be a spice in me of the snuff-taker's vice, love of sub-irritation,— mild pugnaciousness. But I don't want to degrade God's creatures and bid them scratch and so far amuse me.

And here—there is no malice in my transition to Ld. Houghton: I know not one, but a multitude of good, gracious acts of his,—my old thirty-years' acquaintance, or friend *à la rigeur*: but for all that, he plays the social game unfairly, —it may be but *dominos,* still if you play, mind the rules,—and he does not mind them. He "dissembles his love and kicks you down stairs" [1] whereat I kick again, and love shines afresh over our hand-shaking. I don't know whether, if I loved thoroughly in return, I should not rebuke myself—"You, you will not forward the good work of mending this excellent person by really kicking like a Roland next time?"

I know the easy self-deception,—how one may indulge spites and revenges, calling them by pretty names all the time: the ditch is on either side the road—for surely it is as vile a ditch one falls into when one reflects that "gentle

---

[1] Perhaps it was right to dissemble your love,
But— why did you kick me down stairs?
John Philip Kemble (1757-1823) in "The Panel."

words are always gain," [1] and it is gentle to pity
this man and find excuse for the other—instead
of "being angry and sinning *not*." [2]

You shall take me in hand and teach me—if
you don't get tired.

I ought to have gone out this long, not unpleasant day,—and the dark is beginning.

God bless you.

R. B.

November 1st, 1864
Manchester

No, you will not see me next Sunday. I am
not turning my face southwards quite so soon as
I expected, finding more appreciation of my
company here than might have been looked for
in a poor blind world that lets so much excellence slip by! Poor Miss Cobbe! I think I may
excuse myself from reading her, by your account. I shd think you must have derived some
entertainment from your own appearance in
Italian books of travels; as I did the other day
when I came upon a woodcut in a collection of
portraits, which needed the two words under-

---

[1] Tennyson's "Love thou thy Land," line 23; first published in
Poems, 1842, vol. 1, p. 223.

[2] Be ye angry, and sin not. (Ephesians, iv, 26.)

neath to tell me who the ardent youth might be. I suppose Miss C.'s portraits are done much in that style. Oh, if we women knew when to hold our tongues! There is my petition to the gods if ever they shew themselves disposed to grant any of mine. However, as we all talk together it comes to much the same thing as if we were all silent; certainly no pair of ears keep our words long—verily I fear we must have been guilty of a miniature Tower of Babel and are punished with a new confusion of tongues.

You pique my curiosity to see your Helix— no, I know he does not sting you, perhaps it wd be as well if he did. You care, at least, little enough about the opinion of your fellow creatures. I wish with all my heart I could make over some of the vast surplus of that caring from my mind to yours!—one of us at least wd be benefited by the transfer.

Poor Lord Houghton! I think you are ungrateful to him, for you go on from your love of sub-irritation to complain of his dissembling his love and so affording you an excellent opportunity for exercising yours—why may not that be the final cause of his being? Well, I hope it is not the final cause of mine, for I hate the element of even the mildest pugnaciousness

—No, I think we shd never provoke each other.
If that disaster comes to pass I may console myself with the reflection that I am supplying you
with a pinch of snuff, but that is a habit I particularly disapprove and I hope I may do nothing to encourage it. I have a weakness for Lord
Houghton, there seems to me something manqué
about him, which always draws me towards people. I think in those odd omnium gatherum
collections of his there is such a curious kind of
aspiration after excellence in one walk or another, and then he is content to be 2nd rate
himself, which very few people are. I don't
know him socially, so I can't estimate him that
way.

I came upon some of those "Sonnets from the
Portuguese" the other day in an old "Black-
wood,"—you ought to have taken that review to
leave a good taste after the "Edinburgh." But
indeed there is a marvellous readiness to praise
as soon as the object is beyond the reach of
whatever faint pleasure reviews may give! They
are wonderfully beautiful (I don't mean reviews!). I do not know any utterance that has
the same sort of thrill in it as they have—not
that others have not felt it, but it is rarely given
to express and experience at once that sort of

feeling. Generally the life and the art are two things; at least, it seems to me an exception when they are so much one as they were with her.

I hope you are very busy and that I am to see some fruit of it before long. I want to make the most of your declining years. I was so much amused the other day by that old Aunt of mine I told you of who enjoys attacking all my friends, as it is very easy to make me angry that way—when I was with her she found out a curious new sin of yours that you had written "so much."—I hope that sin is to grow worse and that you are to give your Helix many a flower to crawl over yet. Well, I doubt whether we can classify our fellow creatures in that way!

By the bye, what do you think of Tennyson's arrogance about his "little flower"? *All* have got the seed forsooth! [1]—so everybody has strained their ear to catch his cadence! I hope you don't like "Aylmer's Field"—or understand that extraordinary bosh about the singer's

---

[1] Read my little fable:
    He that runs may read.
  Most can raise the flowers now,
    For all have got the seed.
            "The Flower," stanza 5.
  But to appreciate Miss Wedgwood's objection the whole poem should be read. It appeared in the *Enoch Arden* volume, 1864. Browning, writing to Tennyson on the 13th of October, 1864, regarded this "flower-apologue" from a different point of view; see his son's *Memoir,* vol. II, page 16.

wife. I have heard one or two provoking little things of him since I came here. What a strange thing it is that a great man may be vain. I shd have said that was the one quality that cd not go with greatness—but all my theories are being knocked to pieces.

Have you begun dining out again? I suppose dinners are being eaten again though I hear nothing of them. I think it is just a year since you came to our house so ailing—do you remember? You earned great praise on that occasion. I hope your dinners are more propitious now.

Farewell, dear friend.

Ever yrs affly,

F. J. W.

Friday Mg.

Nor *next* Sunday, I suppose, by the wearing away of the week, and no new word to me.

Yes, that was a strange, heavy crown, that wreath of Sonnets, put on me one morning unawares, three years after it had been twined,— all this delay, because I happened early to say something against putting one's loves into verse: then again, I said something else on the other side, one evening at Lucca,—and next morning she said hesitatingly "Do you know I once wrote some poems about *you?*"—and then—"There they are, if you care to see them,"—and there was the little Book I have here—with the last Sonnet dated two days before our marriage. How I see the gesture, and hear the tones,—and, for the matter of that, see the window at which I was standing, with the tall mimosa in front, and little church-court to the right. Afterward the publishing [1] them was through me—in the interest of the poet, I chose that they should be added to the other works, not minding the undue glory to me, if the fact should become transparent: there was a trial at covering it a little by leaving out one sonnet which had plainly a connexion with the former works: but it was put in afterwards when people chose to pull down the mask which, in old days, people used to respect at a masquerade. But I never cared. "The Portuguese"—purposely an ambiguous title—was that Caterina who left Camoens the riband from her hair.

Come, we will—that is, *I* will—be good now

---

[1] "Sonnets from the Portuguese" were published in Mr. Browning's works in 1850: second edition of *Poems*, 2 volumes, Chapman and Hall. The "one sonnet" to which Browning refers is that entitled "Future and Past"; it was printed on the last page of the 1850 collection, and took its place as number 42 of the series when the fourth two volume edition of *Poems* was published in 1856.

and henceforth, as children and the Italians say, and Houghton shall be in the right ten times over: and as for the review, so infinitely viler a one has come out since as to divert my attention from it effectually—the writer beginning his performance by apprising us that we find "the imaginative faculty" in this man and that, and—"here and there a little of it in———Coleridge!" Then he goes on to laud me,—and *him*, you will peradventure allow me to kick "morally," as Leigh Hunt's son used to describe his father's [1] exploits that way.

Oh yes—that dinner, and your administration of ice! Do you know, I was rather resolute against—not pain, but the stupidity which accompanies it: but I knew you were all kind; and did not want to cut a figure colloquially. I shall not go out so much this next time, if it can be helped—feeling headachy already.

Goodbye, dear friend,

R. BROWNING

---

[1] Leigh Hunt's views, on which his oppugnancy was based, are stated by his son Thornton at the beginning of the second volume of *The Correspondence of Leigh Hunt*, Smith, Elder and Company, 1862.

1 Cumberland Place,
Regent's Park, N.W.
Friday, Nov. 18th, '64

Your last letter, which followed me here (for I returned suddenly sooner than I expected) was a very precious one to me. I had been thinking much of its subject—for I had been reading that mention of Miss Cobbe's and it had wrought itself into a curious realistic dream in which I met you both at a theatre, and the double mirage seemed so much more natural than the single. More natural and more true, for I know that you are never alone.

I was looking today at that Threnody of Emerson's [1] that you praised to me in July. There is a great deal that is very beautiful in it. I suppose if any soul could utter the love which has been sealed and sanctified by Death, we should need nothing more for the highest poetry; but I dislike the paganism in that and so much other poetry of that kind. The implied Hades that casts its shade over the thoughts of the lost. I know that it does not fall upon *your* grave and that for you there has only been a working dress laid aside, precious to you, but not precious to

---

[1] Ralph Waldo Emerson (1803-1882), essayist and poet.

the wearer. This has been your rare privilege, that you had the wearer, and not as most of us, only the garment. I do not mean that there is not the infinite in every soul, but so few of us can reach it—we see nothing but the pattern on the veil!

Yes, I am glad you rescued those Sonnets. I have just been reading over the last, which has a sort of tone of repose in it that indicates the date you give it—not that repose is the word, but you will understand what I mean by it.

Dear friend, I trust that for you the lamp that shines through those sonnets is bright enough in the past to keep your present clear and—no, not *bright,* but something removed from the frosty twilight that is the lot of the larger half of this poor world. You had no claim to be exempted from the lot of the rest of us, but I think —nay, I am sure that it has come to you in the form that you can best bear it, as you have not had to see her suffer and you know that God can make up to her for even this short loss of you, if indeed the loss is not merely yours and she is not much closer to you than she ever was— as I think.

Miss Cobbe has had one effect upon me which wd surprise you and her about equally, I shd think, in raising my opinion of your tolerance, which, to tell the truth, could well afford to be raised. It is not a delicate touch in her sketch of your Wife, though there is every intention to be respectful. Well, we are not quite so far gone as the Americans in the habit of speaking of anyone who has written books as if they had forfeited all right to keep the veil down, which is a heresy I particularly dislike, and I shd suppose you must detest it still more. I got hold of the "Edinburgh Review" [1] the other day and tried your pinch of snuff. I was much amused by a good deal of it. You see, they anticipate my great work of commentaries! What lengthy Scholia they will have to be if all things are to be made plain to the Reviewer. My friends make a little preparatory public for me—not being much in your line and yet not being content to let you alone. When am I to see your Italian heroine? I hope you are going to spend with her the time you take from dinners this winter. I am sorry going out does not suit you, but it is a very headachy amusement; perhaps you will demur to the last word! Goodbye, dear friend.

Ever yr affly,

F. J. W.

_____

[1] See note 1, page 93.

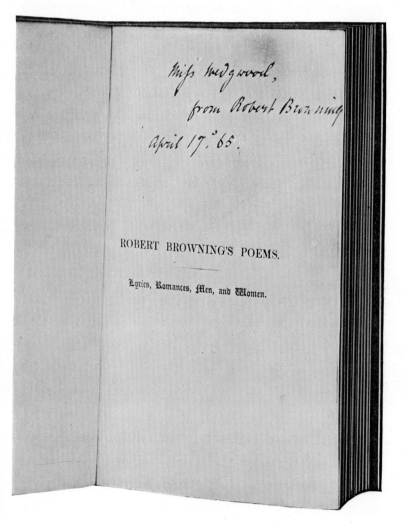

Miss Wedgwood,
    from Robert Browning
April 17.º 65.

ROBERT BROWNING'S POEMS.

Lyrics, Romances, Men, and Women.

ONE OF A NUMBER OF BOOKS PRESENTED TO
JULIA WEDGWOOD BY BROWNING

You must know, that I find myself so out of sorts with a cold and cough, that it is plainly better to keep in the house to-day: the more, that to-night I cannot keep in it, having to dine with my old friend, as I told you. He likes my presence rather than my absence—but I won't be sure that he likes myself rather than my presence. But *you* may, although you are no old friend: so, I reserve my precious being for other Sunday mornings—I thought I would try and go, till the last minute—*now*, when I reluctantly give up the notion. Besides, I fancy colds are "catching,"—and why should you be caught?

I sent the book [1] yesterday.

So, till next Sunday, goodbye!

Yours affectionately,

R. BROWNING

Christmas Day, '64. 2¾ p.m.

Xmas Day, 1864
Cumberland Place

I have been spending this evening with Rabbi-Ben-Ezra—with the "Saturday Review's" opin-

---

[1] No book presented by Browning to Miss Wedgwood on this date has been found. But an inscribed copy of his wife's *Last Poems* was presented on July 7, 1864; of the four-volume edition of her *Poems* (sixth edition, 1864) and of *The Great Christian Poets and the English Poets* on July 13, 1864; and of the three-volume edition of his own *Poems* (fourth edition, 1865) on April 15, 1865.

ion on Rabbi Perida's [1] style for sauce—and must write my line of thanks to the last-named Rabbi for giving me that good omen on this sad Christmas Day. The other Rabbi wd almost convert one to grow old cheerfully, and I need conversion to that doctrine, so it was well to have him to study on the memorial day that comes encrusted with so many old memories. I know that to you one day hardly brings back more than another, for I doubt not you have recollections enough to clothe all the 365.

I shall put my dear book by the little green books where I think he will be very happy and out the way of all despised "Edinburgh-ites." When shall I have his younger sister to keep him company? I do not fancy I shall care for her quite so much as for him, but in saying that I don't at all mean to give up my claim on an early introduction to her. I could wish a few more stitches had been taken up here and there, even still—but I carefully avoid any dissertation on the subject, which I know is transferred from the table to the highest shelf of yr mind, and not to be taken down again on any account.

How spiteful you wd think me if I were to wish you many Xmas's! Yet I believe that is rather

[1] Perida-Browning; see page 38.

my feeling—but I won't put up any prayers for your life to be prolonged till yr "Edinburgh" reviewer finds you a lucid writer. I will be quite content with the 30 years of life which is fairly owing you still according to your own estimate, in which time I expect the rest of yr readers will change their mind as little as I shall about you.

Farewell, dear Perida.

P.S. In spite of your weariness with the subject, I shall make the remark that it seems to me an artistic fault to put James Lee [1] into such a proletarian, to use the horrid new slang, background. Those are not the feelings of people who are earning their bread. I suppose you meant to escape the vulgarity of chateaux, but it gives one a feeling of masquerading to read the complication of those reflections with the slight touches of background. But perhaps there is a fitness in it with some hidden meaning which has escaped the naked eye.

Monday morning.—Your note just come, and yes, certainly, however little I like *you*, I like your presence less, so I am very glad you did not give it me yesterday. As for my not being an old

---

[1] "James Lee" in *Dramatis Personæ*, 1864; in the collected edition, four years later, the title was changed to "James Lee's Wife" and two important personages were added.

friend, that depends which way you read the relationship which of us is subject and which object. I am sorry to hear of your cough, but you must expect to be visited by the infirmities of advancing life, in every sense you are an old friend to

yrs ever,
F. J. W.

19 W. C.
Dec. 31, '64

Well, this is to be a long "week," indeed. I had to go to the friend's dinner, and suffered from it so as to have kept the house the next four days. I am much better now: thank you for writing the other note as well as this.

I only sent the single book, and not the collected things, because there's a new edition printing,—the last I shall scratch commas out of,— and so the fitter for the shelf.

If by any chance you don't return before next Sunday—since to-morrow is to be abolished— please tell me.

Affectionately yours ever,
R. BROWNING

You are quite right in your criticism [1]—since I misled you into thinking the couple were "proletaire"—but I meant them for just the opposite —people newly-married, trying to realize a dream of being sufficient to each other, in a foreign land (where you can try such an experiment) and finding it break up,—the man being *tired* first,—and tired precisely of the love:— but I have expressed it all insufficiently, and will break the chain up, one day, and leave so many separate little round rings to roll each its way, if it can.

Saturday, Jan 7th, '65
Cumberland Place

Tomorrow is to be abolished too, though I am writing here, for I am to spend Sunday with relations elsewhere. I shd like to hear meantime that you are quite well and not only better.

I think on your own shewing yr lovers make a very moral tale, which, I fear, was the last thing you intended: people who without a good cause took up such a life wd deserve that most tragic ending of getting tired of each other's love—though with a good cause I can imagine

---

[1] i.e. of "James Lee," see page 107 and note 1.

the best of life in store for them. See how I shall improve you when my time comes!—do you think you shall enjoy reading me in Purgatory? Send me one line here to say you are not going to make that journey just yet. I have been living in the midst of anxiety and am grown fanciful.

Yrs ever,
F. J. W.

Monday, Jan. 9, '65

Do you know, I may begin to dislike getting letters from you, if they are always bearers of bad news in this way? Never mind, let us see what next Sunday brings with it. I am much better, not altogether well—that's the fact: but there is little amiss. I passed the Park-gate yesterday.

Here is exactly the "line" you ask for: it is a busy day with me—but five more of them, and, the long hours of the Public past, please providence that kindly caters for the sparrow, there shall be champagne and chicken at last—if you continue to "treat," in your goodness,

Yours hungrily and thirstily ever,
ROBERT BROWNING

(Hasn't Perida just got some nice tall fellow to take his part in this "Saturday Review!" [1])

Feb. 10th, 1865
Cumberland Place

I am so sorry, dear friend, to think of even such a slight malady in your house. Yes, we have all had it, but I think you shall not come for a week or two.

We are the centre of a large clan of young cousins running in and out and it is well to be cautious. I am sorry your boy has managed to put it off so late, as it is always worse with the age. I cannot bear to think of all that illness—even the most trifling—must recall to you. Perhaps the more trifling, the more overwhelming in association, for all anxiety drags one's thoughts too imperiously into the future to leave much energy for the past; but the slight occasions of life seem made to be steeped in association; and all illness, especially, must wake to peculiar vividness what never slumbers with you. But I know that your past is mirrored in your future, and the mere edge of land that divides the blue sky from the blue sea is small.

---

[1] The "Saturday Review," January 7, 1865, pp. 15-17, devoted three and a half columns to reviewing the "Edinburgh Review's" notice of Browning; see note 4, page 87.

I was thinking of you the other day in looking at a photograph of your poor old Lear and hearing more of his horrible children. Poor old man! I am afraid there was no heaven in *his* past to be reflected in his future.

I wonder if you will be dined to death before I see you again. I shall compose an Ode on the sad occasion, or don't you think one might make it into an Epigram? as was the "Quarterly" to Keats, etc. (please don't tell me the "Q." never killed Keats, I hate having the old legends disturbed)—so whether we love, or whether we hate we kill all the same.

Farewell, dear friend

Saturday Eg.
(1865)

I know you will like to hear that the boy is quite well, and, since many days, going about his work as usual: the illness began, so far as one could see, and ended in three days—altogether a capital case, said the doctor, who took his leave a week ago. The risk is *now*—exposure to cold would bring on serious disorders: but we shall take care. I was long ago enjoined

Saturday 29.
1865

I know you will like to hear that the boy is
quite well, and, since many days, going about
his work as usual: the illness began, — so far
as one could see, — & ended in three days, — altogether
a capital case, said the doctor — who took his
leave a week ago. The risk is now — exposure
to cold would bring on serious disorders — he
must take care. I was long ago enjoined
to cast aside fears of infecting people — myself — the infection not being transmissible
by other than the patient, — unlike in
this to scarlet fever &c. That is the fact, — but
should not go to you yet, all the same.

    What you said about Keats, in truer

them as you say it = because I believe he
did have truth accelerated, if not indu-
ring that criticism. He did not put forth
in eye, nor bully — bad certainly felt
strongly, what we feel strongly: don't
believe a man of average sensibility is
ever insulted by a blackguard without
suffering enough: despise it? yes, — but
you feel the slap in the face, too: and, in
this case, to feel anything unduly, is
to spoil the post. Opening life = "the
seeds of death were in him already", say
the foolish people: — why quicken them
under a melon-glass then? Both, his

personal discomforts were infinitely increased - that is, his death was hastened -
by poverty: he had terrible fears, wanted
to go abroad as ship-surgeon, to write
reviews, anything to get money and
keep off want & indebtedness: this
came, or was not hindered coming, by
the criticism which stopped the sale of
his books - what poor fraction could
have fallen to his share, when, at least
six years after his death, I sent to his
publisher and got a copy of each
first edition? - no second having
been called for even then: lastly, from

when Severn told me, his irritability
at last almost amounted to madness,
— don't suppose that joking about such
a person's pestle & mortar, & so on, did
not drop well-fire on the sore-place.

Good-bye = it would do you no harm
to write to me, since my epistle is
like to be long, mine pure & me.

Easter-day, I dined where they were
talking about the Davenport Brothers:
said the daughter of our host, "I always
think of the Plymouth Brethren — which
are they?" — "A religious sect". — "Oh,
— and what are the Yarmouth Bloaters"
— "Plainly the salt of the earth" said
            Yours affectionately ever
            Robert Browning.

to cast aside fear of infecting people *myself*—the infection not being transmissible by other than the patient—unlike in this to scarlet fever, etc. That is the fact; but I shall not go to you yet, all the same.

What you said about Keats, is truer than as you say it: because I believe Keats *did* have death accelerated, if not induced, by that criticism. He did not put finger in eye, nor bully—but certainly felt strongly, what we feel strongly: don't believe a man of average sensibility is ever insulted by a blackguard without suffering enough: despise it? yes, but you feel the slap in the face, too: and, in this case, to feel anything unduly, was to spill the fast-lessening life: "the seeds of death were in him already" say the foolish people:—why quicken them under a melon-glass then? Next, his personal discomforts were infinitely increased—that is, his death was hastened—by poverty: he had terrible fears, wanted to go abroad as ship-surgeon, to write reviews, anything to get money and keep off want and indebtedness: this came, or was not hindered coming, by the criticism which stopped the sale of his books—what poor fraction *could* have fallen to his share, when, at least six years after his death,[1] I sent to his publisher and got a copy of each first edition?—no second having been called for even then: lastly, from what Severn told me, his irritability at last almost amounted to madness. Don't suppose that joking about such a person's pestle and mortar and so on did not drop hell fire on the sore-place.

Good-bye: it would do you no harm to write me, since my exile is like to be long, *mi pari a me.*

Yesterday, I dined where they were talking about the Davenport Brothers:[2] said the daughter of our host, "I always think of the Plymouth Brethren—what are they?"—"A religious sect."—"Oh,—and what are the Yarmouth Bloaters?"—"Plainly the salt of the earth" said

Yours affectionately ever,

ROBERT BROWNING

---

[1] Six years after Keats' death Browning would have been fifteen or sixteen; it is good to know that he was interested in Keats at so early an age.

[2] The Davenport Brothers were two high priests of "spiritualism" from America; a biography of them by T. L. Nichols, M.D., was published by Saunders, Otley & Co., in 1864.

Friday, Feb. 24th, '65
I Cumberland Place,
Regent's Park, N.W.

Thank you very much, dear friend, for writing to tell me about yr boy. I wanted very much to hear and shd have been still more anxious but that I had gone to Mrs Procter to ask about him. I am so greatly relieved to think that he is well again, for it is not always a trifling disorder when a person is so nearly grown-up; still more I am glad for you to be spared the associations of illness. All the year I have been feeling as if there were no other sorrow in the world but that of a parent for a child, and so one trembles at the faint possibility of an approach to it for any one.

I have been trying to read Keats since your letter, but I find all gods and goddesses unendurable. This is really, I suppose, not caring for poetry at all, which is form and not substance, and I fear that is my case! I can just put up with Virgil's semi-demi belief in the old mythology, but I can't get below his twilight into our broad day.

Did you ever know Thorwaldsen [1] in Rome?

---

[1] Albert Bertel Thorwaldsen (1770-1844), Danish Sculptor, who arrived in Rome in 1797 and finally returned to Denmark in 1837. Browning first visited Italy in 1838.

What an unpleasing specimen of an Artist he seems to have been!—No, I think I am extending your years even beyond their long span; see what an impression of wisdom you must have made upon me and beware how you imperil it! I have more patience with (or rather I suppose understanding of) the antique in marble, and always had an admiration for him as an artist, which I was sorry to join on to such an objection to him as a man. That was a stupid criticism of his Mercury in the "Saturday Review"—he is resting his hand on the sword, not drawing it. We have the statuette on our chimney piece, so I have a fund of opinion on the subject, which I shd just have liked to make the "Saturday" writer listen to; it wd have made his moral criticisms much more telling to have appreciated the act of the man. But I think 'twas writ by a Woolmister[1] and that sect is not tolerant, though the founder I shd think was—oh no, I remember a dinner here which produced eminently the reverse of tolerance from him. Farewell, dear friend.

Ever affly yrs,
F. J. W.

---

[1] This word is not clear.

1 Cumberland Place,
Regent's Park, N.W.
March 1st, 1865

[1] I have been intending to write to you for several days, dear friend, to say—what I do not say willingly—that it would be better that we did not meet again just now, at least that you did not come here. I have such confidence in your unselfish kindness that I believe I may say this and no more, and you would withdraw from me only what I ask you to withdraw, leaving me the kindly feeling in the consciousness of which I can face a loss that is not small. But I feel a great desire for something more than the friendly acquiescence which I know I should have from you at any rate. I want your sympathy, the support of your longer experience and more matured judgment, and so I tell you the simple truth, which yet could hardly be said to anyone else without risk of misconception—that I have reason to know that my pleasure in your company has had an interpretation put upon it that I ought not to allow. I have no doubt the fault has been mine, in incautiously allowing it to be known that I made an object of your visits. You will

[1] Among Miss Wedgwood's papers two incomplete copies of this letter were found.

feel at once that it is a mistake which must be set right by deeds, not words. I am reflecting on myself, not upon you. You have only accepted a position into which I invited you—remember, I invited you. Your attitude has been response from the beginning. In anything now that I may wish otherwise you have no responsibility. I have drawn it upon myself. It is no use asking myself how far such an opinion would affect me if I had no one to consider but myself. Tell me, am I not now doing what you would wish, if you were in their place? They know that I am the author of all that is peculiar in our intercourse, but I cannot explain this to those others who impute to me anticipations irreconcilable with that fact. I have no reason to think your attitude is misinterpreted but perhaps all the more for this I ought to be careful to correct the view they have of mine. Am I not right, dear friend?

I think it would be affectation in either of us to assume that this can be to one of your age quite what it is to one of mine—still more when one considers that the age of the friendship is so different too, though in another direction. You are to me the friend of years, I only of months to you. Yet I know this is not nothing to you; you will feel as much as I wish about it. Do not exaggerate what it is to me. I have had your sympathy, your friendship, through the darkest part of life. You know in some degree how dark it was, in what a delirium of sorrow I turned to you; you know too, I hope, how fully you satisfied that need. Nothing like that can recur, I believe; some part of it will never depart from me, but there is the temporary in it too, and that grows lighter, and though no friendship ever grows less precious, it—or at least the outward evidence of it—grows less necessary.

Do not think of me. If I did not anticipate this, I at all events took my chance of it. I rejoice to think how much I shall still be able to enter into your mind. I am not anxious at all about the way you will take this, yet I want a letter from you to say what I know you will say, that you are *with* me in it. I do not mean that you see all the involved reasons that there are for my surrendering so much; that is not necessary, as I put no onus of decision upon you, but I mean that knowing that *I* see them, you think me right at whatever cost to undo my own work. Let me soon have that full major chord to content my ear, which can be satisfied afterwards with silence—though if you can still let me see what you promised it will be an even greater pleasure to me than it would have been while I was in the habit of seeing you.

Dear friend, I spin out my letter in reluctance to say goodbye, but it must be said—you know all that it means from me, all you have been to me and how my thoughts will twine round you and yours—and yet you know, too, that I am not giving up more than I can afford; you must believe both facts; it would pain me almost equally that you cd doubt either.   And so you will strip away almost all the pain of this last goodbye for your ever grateful,

F. J. W.

My dear friend, this comes to me as no surprise: I thought from the beginning it was too good to last, and felt as one does in a garden one has entered by an open door,—people fancy you mean to steal flowers.   I consider you are altogether right in deciding *so*—and certainly you are right in being sure that I understand you. I shall talk not another word about it: I "withdraw"—beyond my visits—exactly as much of my appreciation of you—as, having to go to the house no more, I withdraw my knowledge of in what part of London it is situated and whether it look out on trees or a brick wall. What I knew, I know and shall always know, and after this world, I hope, when completion ought to be. As to the past, it was only incomplete thro' my wife's absence: she never had any woman-friend so entirely fit for her as you would have been—I have told you so sometimes.

I like clearly-defined situations and relations, and by temper am led to call for them abruptly and at any price: consequently I bring myself to check this temper, and be moderate in the courses it would induce. I left you always to decide (as only yourself could) on what length into the garden I might go: and I still leave it to you. But I would remark—as common sense must, I think—that to snap our outward intercourse off short and sharp will hardly cure the evil, whatever it be: two persons who suddenly unclasp arms and start off in opposite directions look terribly intimate. But you know all the circumstances.

I shall no more say or hear you say "good-bye" than I said anything of the kind because I kept away when measles were to be apprehended: "not a bit apprehended" said the learned and laughed—but I minded worthy folks' fears: here is a fear of another juvenile ailment, and I may have to keep away long, longer and longest: what then? The old clothes will end in being burned, and then we will shake hands again.

Therefore, no goodbye! But, out of sight or in it, there will never come a change to my impression of you: and it is with no particular emphasis that I bid God bless you, my dearest friend.

Of course, I will send you the poem,[1] when it is done; that can hardly be till next year, however hard I work—and I do work unintermittingly. I shall also send the new edition of my old things—only not, perhaps the very week or fortnight in which it is published—this, for a reason not worth explaining—a printer's reason; your copy will be a little the better.

Ever yours affectionately,
ROBERT BROWNING

Come, we will leave off and go about the week-day work with a laugh, which yet shall be to the purpose. I had a letter from America two days ago,—on opening which, a photograph dropped out. "What can it be?" said I: a youngish man, dressed strangely in a long coat or chlamys, and bare sandalled feet—yet with a

---

[1] *The Ring and the Book*, not published until 1868-1869.

mediæval *juste-au-corps* and the other habiliments—sits alone in a bare room, on a bare bench projecting from a bare wall, save where two masks, tragic and comic, hang in a corner; himself is contemplating a third mask in his hand: he is profoundly melanchody, close shaven, with close-clipped hair, black above a vast brow and lanthorn jaws,—a face like Tasso's,—the mould of his face, which I have seen in the room where he died. Could this be Tasso? Or Iago meditating in a mad-house? Or *what* was the really striking and suggestive little thing? Oh, ye correct comprehenders of human nature,—whether in the great American nations, of which this a product, or in our own London,—this was—Robert Browning writing his "*Dramatis Personæ*," and intended to figure as "frontispiece to that performance but that it was not ready in time!"

So, why wonder if he wear cap and plume, and have guitar, ribbon and all, in the conception of "other people"?

1 Cumberland Place,
Regent's Park, N.W.
Thursday, Ap. 20th, 1865

Was I glad to see my dear books yesterday, do you think?—not so glad, though, as when I received an MS from the same hand a week or two ago which I wanted to write at once and thank you for, but thought it better to wait till I had the larger help of yr writing, though it cannot for me quite equal the smaller. But I knew you wd know all the relief and satisfaction that wd come to me with your letter—yes, relief, for I knew how near I had come to all misconceptions and distrust—rather of myself than of you—made me doubt whether one cd pass through such a strait and narrow way quite safe from the ditch on each side—but you have given me that deep satisfaction of feeling that it is possible. I think you very clever to understand such a person as I am, which is an intoxicating compliment for you—but you see other people can be obscure as well as you!

Dear friend, I thought I shd have missed you terribly, and I do miss you, but I have not regretted giving up the great pleasure of yr visits, and I shall not. Some parts of our intercourse have been almost the best of life to me—specially when you have spoken of your wife—and these do not pass away. Oh, if she had been here when we met! But I will not be so heartless as to bring in my wish into company with your grief, which must move alone.

I have your photograph now to keep company with hers, and I hope one will find its way to your American friend to enable him to compare the real and ideal. I have felt much tempted to give myself one more sight of the original before we leave town for the summer in 10 days time, but I thought that perhaps my asking you to give it me wd frustrate the object with which I asked you not to come—so I must fill up that need with the 3 volumes.[1] I have put them on the shelf with the green ones that they may be as close together as the two writers always have been in my mind—and always will be, throughout the large part of life in which my thoughts are busy with you. Farewell. I must stop writing—it seems difficult—but you know everything I am saying, I think, before you read it. Heaven guard you from all further sorrow! I do not see that it can give you much that has been as yet withheld.

Yrs ever affly

F. J. W.

----

[1] The collected edition of Browning's *Poems*, published by Chapman and Hall. See note 1, page 105.

19 Warwick Crescent,
Upper Westbourne Terrace, W.
May 17, '67

DEAR MISS WEDGWOOD,

The last time you wrote to me you bade me remember I had offered to show you my Poem [1] before it should be published: it is nearly three years since then, and you may well have changed your mind about caring to see the thing—but I don't suppose so, after all—at any rate, it is for me to say that the poem will probably go to press in the autumn, and I will send you the proofs as I get them: from the way I work, it is not in my power to send a proper transcript, such as should give the thousands of lines a fair chance of being run through—eighteen thousand, so far as I know!—Nobody has seen one of all these—and I mention the length to account for the delay in getting done,—besides there have been spaces of interruption, months at a time. Not that the thing *is* altogether done yet, nor by a good deal, —but I expect four months' work will suffice.

But I talk about it thus prematurely because I get thereby the opportunity of answering, if your kindness permit, a note from Mrs Wedg-

---

[1] *The Ring and the Book.*

wood which embarrasses me somewhat: it is just an invitation to dine,—and I can't resolve to make any banal excuse, nor yet seem fussy and foolish. The truth is best said. I underwent great pain from the sudden interruption of our intercourse three years ago: not having the least notion why that interruption must needs be, then or now, I shrink—altogether for my own sake—from beginning again, without apparent reason, what may be stopped once more as abruptly and as painfully without reason one whit more apparent. You understand me, I know—will you make Mrs Wedgwood understand that I am most grateful for her goodness, and grieved that I cannot—in simple justice to myself—have the gratification she would give me? Indeed, I am sure you will,—and want no formal answer any more than you want the assurance that I am

ever yours,
ROBERT BROWNING

May 17, '67
Cumberland Place

It has given me a lively pleasure to see your handwriting again, dear friend, and to receive your kind offer, though prepared by the fiction that I may well have changed my mind, etc.—in which, but that you added "I don't suppose so", I should be tempted to suspect you had forgotten Captain Absolute's advice not to tell more lies than are necessary! [1]

I wish I might see the MS; you greatly underrate my powers of decyphering obscurities if you suppose them exceeded by a mere printer's devil, and surely the form wd suit the matter all the better if it gave scope for a few hypothetical readings. But I shall be very glad to exercise my ingenuity upon it any way at any time. I have often longed since our last meeting for opportunity and sarcasm to remark on the long delay of the appearance of your Italian, but I consoled myself for wanting the first by the recollection that certainly the last would fail me. Nevertheless I am disappointed not to see you again—but why waste my pen and ink in telling you what you know so well? I did not know my Mother had asked you, so the disappointment is the less. I will tell her what you say—do as you think best, dear friend; I only wish to see you again a long way after wishing things to be just

---

[1] Captain Absolute's advice to his servant in Sheridan's comedy of "The Rivals."

as you like. This is very far from being the case in large matters, happily it is not impossible in such very small ones as all that relates to

yours ever

F. J. W.

I have seen you twice in the street since we parted, but I did not think that a favourable opportunity for my attack!

19 Warwick Crescent,
Upper Westbourne Terrace, W.
Oct. 30, '68

DEAR MISS WEDGWOOD,

From one cause or another, my poem—or rather, part of it—is only ready and readably plain *now:* I sit waiting the revises which are to go to America to-day. It is not necessary to tell you,—beginning with the lowest consideration,—that I was anxious for the help of your opinion, and what more you might choose to give me: *that* will be too late, now, for what is printed and done with. But the hindrances were too much for me, you will believe, without needing that I describe them. The results are that the thing will go forth in four volumes, one a month, beginning next December. But as the Americans chose to insist on printing two in one, I send them the second volume also. My friend Milsand,[1] who visited me last spring, read the first and second *parts* of the first volume: the Publisher [2] and, I believe, his wife, examined the two volumes so as to know how to treat them: nobody else has seen a line: so that I nearly begin as I intended—asking, whether I may send you the said two volumes at any time next week? You will show them to no one—out of your family, I add for form's sake.

Now, I shall have your sympathy, whatever be the appreciation my work meet with; also, if you please to criticise it, I shall be as sure of your honesty: but I may beg—not so much for your courage, as your confidence in my own somewhat stiffish texture of mind, and my ability to bear banging, if you see cause to bestow it. I will endeavour to let you have the remainder of the poem in time to make immediate use of whatever correction of yours I may wish to adopt. Even in the present case, there will presumably be a second edition—and the opportunity I lose now.

[1] Joseph Milsand, French author, whom Browning met in Paris in 1852 and with whom he maintained a warm friendship up to the time of Milsand's death in September, 1886.

[2] George Smith (1824-1901), head of the firm of Smith, Elder and Company.

It is more than a year since I heard from you
—remember, I have no means of knowing that
this application comes inopportunely, should it
do so. You may be absent, too; but this direct
way of writing is better than inquiring through
friends. I trust you are well and that you will
inform me on that point.

Ever yours truly,

ROBERT BROWNING

Thomas Erskine Esq.
Linlathen, Dundee,
Nov. 2, '68

How kind of you to remember me still, dear
Mr Browning. I need hardly say with what delight I shall receive the Volumes [1] (will you send
them me here by post?), which I have looked
for eagerly now for some time. The reading will
form a very helpful distraction to my occupation
here—watching a painful deathbed. I have just
been feeling that I needed some infusion of new
life; now you will give it me, as you have so often
before. I often remember your injunction which,
in this house, I shall have no temptation to

---

[1] *The Ring and the Book.*

break, and will drink my wine in private like the most confirmed drunkard.

I feel dreadfully afraid of the perusal. I so long that this shall be your best gift to the world, as it is to be so much the largest, and are such longings ever satisfied? You, yourself, I know give it the largest share of your approval, but I doubt how much that implies, concave and convex especially so. I know the outline of the story (you told me), but one has a poor judgment of the necklace from the thread.

Your letter gave me some amusement, as well as very much pleasure. I do not often get any one to "play at horses" with me now. Well, we small creatures enjoy it now and then, and lend ourselves to the game with such zest that we deceive ourselves. Perhaps you will find me a good foolometer. No. I retract that perhaps. I cannot believe my understanding of you is any guage of the world's.

I am glad you have had M. Milsand with you— it gives me pleasure to hear of old friends meeting. I wish you had told me that all was well with you and your son. You know how near that welfare lies to the wishes of yours ever,

JULIA WEDGWOOD

19 Warwick Crescent,
upper Westbourne Terrace, W.
Nov. 5, '68

My dear Miss Wedgwood,

With this, or nearly, should be the books—
half of the poem. Do not hurry yourself to report about them (you keep the copy, which may
help, with what part of the new half I shall send
you, to refresh your memory at a doubtful point).
But I think I shall beg you to acknowledge re-
ceipt at once,—that I may know you are not still
waiting for them.

I am here, much as of old. I don't remember
if you know that my Father died two years
ago: [1] my sister [2] (the only one,—I never had a
brother) keeps me company here. My son is
well—just going not to Balliol, alack, as I hoped
would be,—*why* after all?—but to the more
congenial Ch. Church: he will never be an adept
at grammatical niceties, which are the daily bread
at Balliol ——[3] he will lose[4] the other things we
tried to acquire. So, having let the Ch. Ch.
matriculation pass by, this term, he will go up

---

[1] On the 14th of June, 1866, in his 85th year.
[2] Sarianna Browning went to live with her brother after their father's death.
[3] Word illegible.
[4] This word may be "love."

at Christmas. I had to lose Arabel Barrett[1] in June—she died in my arms. This place is *bear-able*—it was never *more* than that. I may stay till the Boy leaves College.

You know, I wish you were in Scotland for any other reason than you give.

What are the conventionalities and decencies? My sister keeps house here, and people come to see her sometimes,—women-people: is the notion that I might see *you*, so—a birth of this memorable Gunpowder-treason-and-plot-day —fraught with fire and brimstone?

Here or there, or wherever I possess my soul, I am, dear friend,

Yours ever,
R. B.

Linlathen, Dundee
Nov. 5, '68

Ah, dear friend, how vain is the attempt to criticise when I hear your voice in my ear again! I will not say my interest stops where others begin—for I feel that at some time I shall care to estimate the creation and lay aside my care for these "indications of the creator." But now I

---

[1] This sister of Mrs. Browning was seven years her junior.

only look for you in your work, and find so much of you that all judgment is quenched as absolutely as when after long exile in some barbarous land one should hear English spoken once more. Ungrateful simile! 'Tis true only at the goal. The book came in too late to acknowledge by this post. Thank you, thank you many times. I always think of you with that word in my heart.

I am so grieved to hear you have lost any one belonged to your beloved one. But the world can hardly grow emptier to you than it was when she left it. I hope that still dearer pledge will be all you need and half you hope. One sentence in your letter saddened me—is your home indeed only bearable? But I understand. It is much if life is bearable sometimes. A grand Bronzino hangs opposite me—a soldier with hand on hip and a strange look of resolute resignation, that I have often met with longing of late. Manly endurance is more and more my ideal of life— womanly endurance is common and so is manly action. How wonderfully I trust to your tracking the underground course of these thoughts which perhaps are hardly worth it. I shall write again, though I believe I shall only repeat the first sentence of this letter. I am your eager listener always,   F. J. W.

I think both halves of me have read your two volumes,[1] dear friend, the half that drinks too eagerly to appreciate the flavour, and the half that sips fastidiously and sometimes makes a wry face.

I am not taken in by your efforts to make me think my words of value. "It is more blessed, etc." I detect your application and thank you, but am content with the other end of the divine paradox—the blessing on the poor. Be content with yours. Still there are some things I want to say, which you will understand and I shall understand, as I say them. Perhaps I am merely indicating my own intellectual limitations; yet if that is all, they are still the limitations, I think, of a fair specimen of the class you address.

You seem to me hardly, if at all, liable in this work to the stock reproach against you; the design is perfectly clear and there are not many details, if any, that are not equally distinct. You give a stereoscopic view (only it is a case of more

---

[1] The first two volumes of *The Ring and the Book*. A set of the four volumes of this poem was found amongst Miss Wedgwood's effects. Though uninscribed by Browning, they were doubtless his gift.

than two eyes, so the simile breaks down) and the solidity is quite satisfactory.

Perhaps this very clearness only brings out the grumble which has always mixed itself with my delight in what you utter. Do you remember once saying to me that your Wife was quite wanting in—I am not sure of the exact words, but the sense was, the scientific interest in evil? —I think you said, the physiology of wrong. I feel as if that interest were in you unduly predominant. I well remember your speaking with strong dissent, with which I entirely sympathized, of that kind of moral science which thinks it can fill up the valleys without lowering the hills. I know the depth of the valleys *is* the height of the hills. I know that we can only discern the white against the black. But hatred and scorn of evil, though it be inseparable from the love of good, ought not surely to predominate over it? I know it does with natural man. One takes the good for granted, one exclaims when it comes to an end, everywhere it is the evil that seems positive. But I look upon the Poet as essentially the *super*natural man and I complain of him when he only mirrors our weakness.

Do you remember Bacon's description of the office of Poetry, in *The Advancement of Learn-*

ing?, "to satisfy the mind" (I forget the exact words) by some shadow of a higher justice than any exhibited in actual life, *"the soul being so much greater than the world."* This is the element I long for more of in you. You seem to me so to hunger for intensity that you lose the sense of proportion whenever you begin to lay on dark shades. Here, for instance, you have one pure, delicate, soft bit of pearly colouring; but the effect is marred, to my mind, by the black being carried up to its very edge, while its area is needlessly restricted.

The picture of a fribble turned to a man— (the "swordless sheath filled [1]," as you put it elsewhere)—by his first contact with a pure spirit, the quick response to purity that begets trust, and that rarely felt, still more rarely conceived, emotion—the most refined, I think, of this earthly experience—when a woman leans upon a man's disinterested tenderness and finds a love that ends with itself—all these things, surely, form the core of what you have to say? So much fringe of blackness as brings out this we accept willingly. We need the atmosphere of meanness and cruelty to exhibit fully the luminous soul that centres the picture. But

---

[1] See Browning's "The Statue and The Bust" 1:15.

surely, surely we have more of this than that small white figure can bear. One's memory seems filled by the despicable husband, the vulgar parents, the brutal cutthroats; the pathetic child is jostled into a corner. I long for more space for her. In the 3rd & 4th vols I hope we shall have it, but still it is not a mere question of the number of printed pages that are occupied with her. There is, what seems to me an absolute superfluity of detail in the hideous portraits, whatever may be bestowed elsewhere. Thersites is brought so fully into the foreground that Achilles can be brought no nearer. It is dangerous to illustrate criticism—very likely any principles of judgment may be wrong, but any illustrations I might bring forward would be still more likely to be so. But, for instance, would not Caponsacchi have touched more lightly on all that was foul while his soul was full of Pompilia? Might not his speech have been free from Swift-like metaphor? An intense pure love does not distance *indignation*—far from it. But that kind of scorn that is mixed with loathing is, I think, wonderfully silenced in its neighbourhood. Would not the narratives of the Crucifixion lose—I do not say grace or beauty but actually *force*, by any elaboration of

the character of Judas? I feel it even in that
allusion in the *Acts*. The Evangelists were not
pleading for their Master before a second Pilate,
you may say. Still I think the hypothetical
change brings forcibly before one's mind the
power of *perfectly* unselfish love (where it is im-
perfect the effect is sometimes directly opposite)
to avert its eye from all evil.

I feel sometimes tempted to be indignant with
you for this, because it seems to me you are so
bound to give us this which we need. Do you
know what an exceptional experience yours has
been? I think sometimes the exceptional element in our own fate is hidden from us. I do
not, thank God, think it anything exceptional
that the power of love should be fully exercised.
Except with a poor soon-crushed Pompilia, for
whom God keeps the good wine till the last, I
believe we are debarred from loving only by our
own faults. But love, to most of us, is quite as
much the discipline, as the refreshment, of life.
We would give our lives for those whose presence
is a continual scourge to our taste, or we watch
hungrily for the footsteps of those of whose lives
we can only think with a blush. Or we de-
liberately choose companions—perfectly satisfactory to a part of our nature perhaps, but

utterly unresponsive to so much, that the joint life seems a starved poor mutilated thing. Does not almost every marriage illustrate some form of this dislocation? But your love had not to split itself up into gratified taste in one direction, and exercised severance in another and intellectual sympathy in a third. One channel held them all.

Did you not thereby contract this debt to us to give some intellectual translation of your experience, and make us feel that love is the principle thing in this world and the world beyond. Oh, do not leave *scorn* in that prominent rivalry with it! There are more things I should like to say, but I have a notion I have tired out my hearer's patience! I should like to ask why you break down the dramatic framework so often in your characters? That passage about Justinian and the Pendects, for instance, is yours and not Franchescini's. But you must have a distinct intention in this and I can't help always enjoying it, it seems so characteristic of you— though it does seem to me an artistic defect.

I had marked some lines to suggest to you as sounding rugged to my ear, but you must have intended that effect, I think. I can't tell you how wonderfully subtle some touches of Pompilia seem to me. I feel as if they must be a real woman's words. The speech about the *pain of womanliness* is to me a wonderful revelation of apprehension of *our* side of the question, which I can meet with no correlative intuition into yours. I can't imagine what corresponds to it—whether anything corresponds to it. A consciousness of limitation somewhere, I suppose, but I cannot guess where.

Dear old friend, to whom I am no old friend, but glaringly modern, let me have one word in answer to this. If it seems to you hopeless and futile misapprehension, still resolve this diminished seventh which has spread itself all over the instrument, and you can satisfy with three fingers. You know how intensely I listen for all your utterances; if you see nothing else in this letter take it as a clumsy expression of that. I shd like to know that life is not all arid to you. But you have your son—and surely much true friendship, even as warm and unchanging as that of

yrs ever affectionately,
JULIA WEDGWOOD

I have written at night; the daylight hours are spent in the sick room. I mention it as an

excuse for diffuseness.   One wants time to con-
dense.

19 Warwick Crescent,
Upper Westbourne Terrace, W.
Nov. 19, '68

I will promise never to spare you of my
gratitude if you engage never to doubt whether
I think your gifts true gold.   It ought to be so,
between us.   But if you won't *begin* by leaving
off, *I* won't (child-fashion), so I formally tell
you I value your criticism, over and above its
being an utterance of yours, beyond what words
are likely to make you believe.   In this case, I
think you do correctly indicate a fault of my
nature—not perhaps a fault in this particular
work, artistically regarded: I believe I do unduly
like the study of morbid cases of the soul,—and
I will try and get over that taste in future works;
because, even if I still think that mine was the
proper way to treat this particular subject,—the
objection still holds, "Why prefer this sort of
subject?"—as my conscience lets me know
I do.

Come, next time I will try in other directions.
But here,—given the subject, I cannot but still

· 143 ·

say, given the treatment too: the business has been, as I specify, to explain *fact*—and the fact is what you see and, worse, are to see. The question with me has never been "Could not one, by changing the factors work out the sum to better result?," but declare and prove the actual result, and there an end. Before I die, I hope to purely invent something,—here my pride was concerned to invent nothing: the minutest circumstance that denotes character is *true:* the black is so much—the white, no more. You are quite justified perhaps in saying "Let all that black alone"—but, touching it at all, so much of it must be. I have made the most of every whitish tint in the thing's texture: and as, when Northcote asked Reynolds why he put no red into his flesh, looked awhile earnestly at his own hand and then replied, "I see no red here"—so I say, "I see no more white than I give."

But remember, first that this is God's world, as he made it for reasons of his own, and that to change its conditions is not to account for them —as you will presently find me try to do. I was struck with the enormous wickedness and weakness of the main composition of the piece, and with the incidental evolution of good thereby,— good to the priest, to the poor girl, to the old

Pope, who judges anon, and, I would fain hope, to who reads and applies my reasoning to his own experience, which is not likely to fail him. The curious depth below depth of depravity here—in this chance lump taken as a sample of the soil—might well have warned another from spreading it out,—but I thought that, since I could do it, and even liked to do it, my affair it was rather than another's.

Just see—you who think I might have lightened the load of bistre—Guido and the four cutthroats did their murder: well? and what more could they do? Why,—(as, depend on it, you are to hear in good or bad time!) Guido's first thought during the flight was, "Why pay these the money I promised,—which they will never dare claim?" And he would not pay them,—while flying for his life; and they? Behind his back they snatched counsel, each of the other, "Since he cheats us,—why not kill him and get his money?"—and so all four at once agreed to do: so that, had he not been arrested in his first sleep, Guido would have never awakened at all, since they meant, on their own awakening, to murder him. Again, the Convertites who harboured Pompilia, are you prepared for what they did, immediately after her death, and continued doing when her innocence had been made apparent to the world? They laid claim to all her wealth, declared themselves her heirs to the detriment of her child, "seeing that all dishonest women consigned to their keeping forfeited to them, in the event of their death while so superintended, whatever property they might have": hence, Pompilia having been nominally given to them as a dishonest woman, they caught at her money with tooth and nail— so that they could only be disengaged by a regular decree of the tribunal that Pompilia, having been altogether innocent, they must let her alone. No, you must fall back on the other charge,—"Why not let all this horror alone?"

The worst is, I can promise you nothing better in what follows: unless the Pope's Judgment (longest book in the poem) come in as a new light: I did mean it should be so, however. The next book, Pompilia, is all white too: but then come the two buffoon lawyers, and, after the Pope, you have Guido's last display—not pleasant certainly. Also the Augustinian preaches a sermon and the priest has a final word to add in his old age. "I can no more"—as dying operatic heroes sing.

The coarseness—ay, but the man is Italian,

noble, and living in 1698, and speaking not to the woman, but against her enemies: all *great* (conventionally great) Italians are coarse— showing their power in obliging you to accept their cynicism. Why is the allusion to Justinian *mine* and not the man's I give it to? The whole of his speech, as I premise, is untrue—cant and cleverness—as you see when the second speech comes: but he was quite able to cant, and also know something of the Pandects, which are the basis of actual Italian law. What are the other escapes from dramatic propriety into my own peculiar self—do tell me that! But I must leave off. So do not you, but continue to help me. I seem not to have begun, even, to say the many things I had in mind to say. Write to me again; your letters will be absolutely alone in the delight they give me.

I leave off to go and dine with Tennyson [1], who goodnaturedly sent this morning to invite me.

Goodbye, Dearest friend,

R. B.

You may see I cannot review what I have scribbled. Forgive it all.

[1] "Br. is coming again tonight to read part of his new poem." Tennyson's letter-diary, November 1868, in his son's *Memoir*, vol. II, p. 59.

Dec. 3rd, '68
Middleton Lodge,
Richmond, Yorks
On my way home

Yes, dear Friend, I fear you do not over-estimate the amount of my divergence. I tried to narrow that angle to include the form alone, but as you see it, the form and matter are inseparable, and you doubtless are right. I wish I could apprehend the attraction of this subject to you. I thought I shared your interest in morbid anatomy. I think our issue lies here. You say, "this is God's world, as he made it for reasons of his own." I demur. Guido seems to me not at all to belong to the world, as God made it. While yet by a strange paradox *that* world wd be exactly the one where Art finds no foothold. It is along the boundary line that its path seems to me to lie—where the waters separate for the two great oceans; on whichever side that watershed is lost sight of, my interest fails. I look to a time when we shall lose sight of the boundary, when this, that we call evil, whether explained or not, shall at all events recede and fade, when we shall partake in God's own calm and need no edge of blackness to tell us what is white. But meantime, in this world any attempt at rendering this seems to me condemned to hopeless futility,—so far I go with you. It is the struggle of two elements, the edge of black and white, that seems to me to teach us the meaning of both. Your curious "depth below depth of depravity" loses sight of this edge. I see no possibility of good in Guido. He seems to me to retain nothing, not only of what God made, but of what—to speak with coarse, superficial conciseness—God can use. Here is no energy of hate, a strong instrument for his displeasure—"hateful to God and to his foes" [1]— one sees no place for such a character on the battlefield.

I think there must be something in the subject to which I am wholly blind, for what I am saying is so obvious; and yet you have chosen it. I shall listen for the old Pope, but except his and Pompilia's utterance I fear I shall not find much food in the remaining books. But, oh, be merciful to us in Guido's last display! Shame and pain and humiliation need the irradiation of hope to be endurable as objects of contem-

---

[1] In *Balaustion's Adventure* Browning has, "Ways harsh to men, hateful to gods, at least!" This poem was not published till 1871, so the lines may possibly be an echo of the ones Miss Wedgwood quotes.

plation; you have no right to associate them in our minds with hopeless, sordid wickedness. Having to meet them so often, to travel with them so large a part of the way, we demand of the teacher that he shall help us to endure their terrible neighbourhood by shewing them as guides towards the light. Do I take too moral a view of the poet's duty? I know you hate this, and I believe I do too. But in this short life, where good fights at such terrible odds with evil—where God hides his face and the Devil shews his—I cannot feel that one of the greatest motive forces we have at our command may rightly act independently of the great battle. We need rest from it—yes, I feel that is the function of Art; it is exactly that the moral sense may go to sleep. But it should awake refreshed.

It was not only in a critical spirit that I complained to myself as I read, for I felt as if I were reading what you had lost in your wife. The sense of good seemed dimmed.

Oh yes, dear Friend, do give us something purely from yourself. Give her a monument more durable than that at Florence—give something that all who read may recognise as the utterance of one who has been taught supremely to believe in goodness by the close neighbour-hood of a beautiful soul. I look yet to recognise the sunshine of her presence in the ripe fruit of your mind. I seem to feel in myself the woman's error—the over-tendency to incarnate all things. Ah, well, take it for what it is worth! She must have been your window, even if you could go out and look direct into the face of Heaven. Now that the window is darkened, you will not forget how the room looked. In no sanc-tuary of Heaven could it be other than keen pain to know that one's gifts were not permanent. What coarse things words are! and perhaps here the meaning is coarse too. Yet I feel as if some rich modulation of harmony or formless melting of colour would best express what I am trying to put into language, and yet perhaps I make a baseless pretence to subtlety in saying so.

I would I knew that I exaggerated the chill-ness and aridity of your present life. The permanent sense of loss I can quite bear to con-template. Adieu, dearest friend. How blessed is the etymology of that word! The love deeper than our deepest absorbs all anxiety—for anxiety is born of impotence.

Ever yrs,
F. J. W.

19 Warwick Crescent,
Upper Westbourne Terrace, W.
Jan. 21, '69

I have delayed sending my next volume—
you well [1] know why! Still, I do send it at last,
though for no bad reason: for, I don't know
how, the sending seems a repetition of the old
cruel joke of the judge, "I sentence you," said
he to an offender, "to be whipped from one end
of the town to the other!"—"Thank you, you
have done your worst!"—"And back again!"
added the judge. So, you have thought the
worst was over,—so, you get this! Accept the
willingness on my part to be wrong, if I could
but get to think myself so, which is no fault of
yours! "I like to be" *(so)* "despised"—quoth
Mawworm [2]: and I take all your blame for better
than other folks' praise.

The worst is, I think myself dreadfully in the
right, all the while, in everything: apart, of
course, from my own incapacities of whatever
kind, I think this *is* the world as it is, and will
be—*here* at least. Shall I dare tell you? I
think that in no energetic deed would you attain

[1] This word may be "will."
[2] Mawworm in Bickerstaff's comedy of "The Hypocrite," Act V,
Scene i.

to a greater general amount of good than you get here,—though the individual qualities (I meant to write, quantities, but my head aches and the afternoon is dark and confounding), the factors in the sum would be different. Think of your first combination, say, of six people, that do any remarkable thing: there will be nobody to match Guido, whose wickedness does . . . or rather, by the end, *shall* . . . rise to the limit conceivable: but is your second better than Pompilia, your third than Caponsacchi, the others than the Pope, and the two old foolish, rather than wicked—people? I mean, that your good will want as much of the goodness of these, one with another, as your bad wants of the wickedness of Guido: then, this good (of my lot) comes through—is evolved by—that prodigy of bad: hence its use, hence my poem, hence your blame, hence my kissing the rod, hence this word to beg you to lay it on again and spare not! The buffoon lawyers (not a bit intellectually and morally beneath lawyers I have known) serve an artistic purpose, and let you breathe a little before the last vial is poured out: Guido "hope?"—do you bid me turn him into that sort of thing? No, indeed! Come, I won't send more, if you will but lift your finger! There, be you as grateful as a lady who, telling me of her trials last week at a dull dinner-party, where people, whom she had counted on meeting, were absent, added, "But justice was tempered with mercy, for So-and-So took me downstairs to dinner!"

Well, I like *knowing,* at any price: also, I like the power that comes of it. "Agnes" ("Where's Agnes?") [1] chose to call on me the other day— I had not seen her for seven years: my wife would not, or could not, know her, and suffered miserably through her ignorance: in half an hour I gained a victory which, could my wife have hoped, even, to do, would have made her happy indeed—and which she could have gained by no effort that I can imagine: it was as easy to me as "kiss my hand"—and not altogether unlike it.

By the way, my wife would have subscribed to every one of your bad opinions of the book: she never took the least interest in the story, so much as to wish to inspect the papers. It seems better so to me, but *is* it better? So, the naturalists say that all female beauties are weaknesses and defects except to the male

---

[1] "Where's Agnes?" is the title of one of Mrs. Browning's *Last Poems,* published by Chapman and Hall in 1862.

creature, and all real beauty is in *him*, if he could but see! Only, he can't.

Goodbye. You must tell me the amount of stripes due this time, however. Surely, poor Pompilia is prettily done—"a half-penny worth of bread to this intolerable quantity of vitriol!"

Ever yours,
R. B.

Jan. 22, '69
I Cumberland Place,
Regent's Park, N.W.

No, I don't know why you have delayed sending the 3rd vol, unless to punish me for impertinence! But I have it now. I must write again when I have read it. I have read yr letter with many a smile. Is he such a bad Economist as to waste good satire on *me?* No, I answered myself, whatever may be his sins, I cannot think quite so ill of his "practical reason." Being emancipated from that coarse theory, which assumes that great souls speak truth, I have a ready alternative. How stupid is our blunder in making the suspicion of fiction an insult! It is the large and generous nature that invents, and who shall say that the fiction may not be a creation? that we may not incarnate a generous hypothesis, so that a Poet becomes an ex post facto Historian? Well, it is a historical fragment in your letter that gave me most lively pleasure. Yet our poor weak nature feeds on fiction too.

All this I write from myself, and yet, I think, a larger half responds, "I like knowing at any price." It is a heavy price sometimes, leaving us penniless. Yet it is a good bargain. You see I adopt your style and send you the two halves of—the antithesis of Rome. Where is the Tertium Quid to find some grain of truth in each? I hate Tertium Quids! I will have both.

Dear Friend, I thank you for some things in your letter from the bottom of my soul. You know what I most care to know about you. It joined on to what else of yours I was reading— the beginning of Pompilia. Yes, it is a lovely Snowdrop growing out of that dunghill, but I can't forgive you for planting it there. No indeed, I vehemently and indignantly deny that half a-dozen of any acquaintance beaten up together wd yield your quantum of badness—not even if I threw you in as one of them!

But that dainty, lovely, pathetic little picture is an exquisite pleasure to me. It seems like some sudden snatch of melody breaking in on the din of tumult and clamour. How wonderfully you understand the woman's nature! No not *wonderfully*—I retract the senseless adverb —most comprehensibly. You will have another letter, dear friend, to read from

yours ever,

F. J. W.

Jan. 30, '69
Cumberland Place

Pray make haste to send me the old Pope to take the taste of the lawyers out of my mouth!

What a strange mixture it is, that you are so strongly and so incompletely dramatic! You have a photographic impartiality of attention that I cannot understand—you lead us through your picture gallery and your stable yard at exactly the same pace, which impartiality is, I suppose, the test of dramatic, as distinguished from mere lyric, feeling. And yet you never really vary the dialect. I shd have thought that very detachment of attention from sympathy wd have implied a filtering away of your own thoughts from your own representations, which is the very opposite of what I find with you.

Do I make any sort of meaning clear? No doubt the very purpose of poetry is to give an intellectual shape to feelings which are, in ordinary minds, mere diffused colour—yet I chafe against the idea that any blot of mud shd afford just as much subject for your pencil as a streak of sunset-remembering in the sky. To bear so much intellectual elaboration feelings ought, it seems to me at least, to be *large*.

It is, I suppose, the consistent dramatic feeling I quarrel with—this readiness to hold a brief for any character or feeling, so it is only individual, to work coldly out any problem, so that it is sufficiently complex without examining the premises. This, I suppose, only shews how narrow and shallow I am. But I am sure the two things together make evil more prominent. I cannot bear to see your thoughts on loan to deck out a sleek pedantic buffoon. When I bring out this edition of your works with which I used to threaten you, I shall only keep enough of Guido and the lawyers to make an ebony frame for that pearly image of Pompilia. Will it not be a terrible punishmnet for you, if you have to read the work in the other world?

But even with Pompilia I feel here and there what I have said—you seem to me to spoil your pearl in cutting it, once or twice. For instance, look at page 73. Surely the death bed narrative of an illiterate girl should be understandable at once. I may be extra stupid, but I cannot make out the construction of the sentence beginning, "I did think, do think," [1] etc. It seems to me as if it wanted a predicate. It must be some stupidity of mine, but surely the fact that it is possible to puzzle over it in reading it carefully is so far a condemnation of the presentment of the character. It seems to me one of the many instances where your thoughts overflow the dramatic channel. "Not this man who, from his own soul, rewrites the obliterated charter" . . . surely that is your idea, not Pompilia's. You said "It is mine too" when I made the remark about Guido, but I always feel in such passages as if I heard the tune on another instrument. It is your lending so much of *yourself* to your contemptible characters makes me so hate them. I cannot endure to hear your voice in those Advocates' pleadings. Certainly you present us with a wonderful variety of mud; the defence is even more hateful than the attack. The impure medium is wonderfully brought out in the con-

---

[1] These words occur actually in p. 72 of volume III of the first edition of *The Ring and the Book.*

trast between that sullied image seen through it and the picture in all its native purity. I can not venture to tell you all that Pompilia seems to me. I felt as if it were only half yours, but indeed I do not divide the other influence from your own.

Dear friend, how one says the insignificant, secondary half of one's thoughts! It is as if all utterance were the postscript to some letter that contained all that one really cared to say—the mere refuse after the valuables had been locked up. I doubt if even my postscript is intelligible, or would be to another. I have a wonderful sense that you can drop some grain into these muddy thoughts, that will make them clear—clearer than they are to myself. It seems arrogant after all these years to expect it, but I cannot help expecting it. I rest with a confidence I can hardly justify to myself on your understanding me—on your having always understood me—and that even if you have half-forgotten me, whatever you remember is just. This is a long way from Pompilia, but this blunt pencil of Language always recalls its own imperfections to one's mind when one wants to draw anything subtle, and I went from one imperfection to another.

This is a long letter to give the most impatient

man in the world to read, as I believe you are, very nearly. Yet it contains nothing but the mere marginal note of my thought. I must not venture on the text, but I think you know it, you will have understood my delight in renewing my acquaintance with your thoughts. Dear friend, farewell.

Y. affec.,
F. J. W.

Feb. 1, '69

I make haste to say, with unfeigned satisfaction, that you are quite right about the faulty passage at page 73—there is a line dropped out . . . of my mind, rather than the M.S., a line I will supply cheerfully, something to the effect that the thought in which P. [1] will die is— that the proximity to such a man as she describes would be an advantage and nothing to blush about. I have made her go on, you see, on the wings of the thought, till it grew sufficient for itself, demonstrative enough of the fact that she would have begun by enunciating. This being a real blunder, I have the privilege of praising myself under the pretence of making excuse—

[1] Pompilia in *The Ring and the Book*.

so, pray you to observe that it has been a particularly weary business to write this whole long work by my dear self—I who used always to be helped by an amanuensis—for, I cannot clearly see what is done, or undone, so long as it is thru' the medium of my own hand-writing—about which there is nothing *sacred*—imperative for, or repellent of—change: in print, or alien charactery, I *see* tolerably well: yet I have had to do all this scribbling, and how much more that you will never see! But I "buckled to," and the thing is done, ill or well: *well*, I think, on the whole.

It is a shame, that when there is anything you contrive to like in it, you cry out, "It's not yours, you know—only half yours," and so on: then comes an ugliness, and "Ah, there you are at home,—there, I see you at work!"—you comment. Unfair,—because, if the good is not mine (as you fancy) in the sense that it is copied from a model,—why may not the uglinesses be copied too, and so not mine neither? I don't admit even your objections to my artistry—the undramatic bits of myself you see peep thro' the disguised people. In that sense, Shakespeare is always undramatic, for he makes his foolish people all clever. I don't think I do more than better their thoughts and instruction, and ¹, up to the general bettering, and intended tone of the whole composition—what one calls, idealization of the characters. What is in the *thought* about the "charter" impossible to Pompilia, if you accept the general elevation of her character? Besides, it is Italian ignorance, quite compatible with extraordinary insight and power of expression too: I have heard abundant instances of it. For the first instance that occurs,—you would not put into the mouth of an English maid, profoundly ignorant, this phrase, "She had a certain nobility of mind which, finding in itself nothing of the base and evil, could not credit their existence in others." Yet that is word for word what Annunziata ² said to me of my wife: "aveva nua certa nobiltà d'animo," etc.

As for the lawyers, why, WHO is going to find fault with me, in the other world, for writing about what *I*, at least, wish had never been made? But made they are, and just so,—apart, as in the other case, from more shrewdness and learning than they are likely to have,—just so, I have known them: in this present instance, you have the very arguments of the very men: Pom-

---

¹ Word illegible.
² The maid who was with the Brownings when Mrs. Browning died.

pilia's all-but-crime was never conceded—far from it—but was invariably afterward *supposed*, just to show how the clever man could bowl *that* down also, were it set up. Indeed, very reluctantly, I left out one prime passage, "spared you" indeed, the fine fellows' notion—illustrated wonderfully—of how far appearances may deceive. I hate the lawyers: and confess to tasting something of the satisfaction, as I emphasize their buffoonery, which was visible (they told me at Balliol, the other day) on the sour face of one Dr Jenkins, whilehome Master of the College, when, having to read prayers, he would of a sudden turn and apostrophize the obnoxious Fellows, all out of the discreet words of the Psalmist, "As for liars, I hate & abhor them!"—then go on quietly with his crooning.

I will, in a sort, go on with mine, by sending you the Pope in a day or two—ah, and Guido's last dying speech and confession, and so relieve me and you!

Now, in another key, "Even if I have half-forgotten you, whatever I remember is just?" Are *you* dramatic here, and who is it supposes I half-forget? I think, on the whole, it is probable we shall never meet again, face to face. Depend on it, I keep what I gained, and shall never part with an atom of it. It was foolish of whoever deprived me of what would have done good to me, and harm to nobody: but good remains, as Pompilia says, and I shall use it up to the end of,

Yours,
R. B.

19 Warwick Crescent,
Upper Westbourne Terrace, W.
Feb. 12, '69

Here is my last trial of your patience, and, as the prayer-book comfortably directs, "In quires and places where they sing, here followeth the anthem"—*I* help to intone it, I know, profoundly tired as I am of the whole business, but not more dissatisfied with my work, and the immediate effect of it, than one should expect.

I shall begin something else in a different way. Do write to me sometimes. I was startled the other day at a house where I dined for the first time,—the Spottiswoodes',—by hearing that "the Wedgwoods" were expected afterward: I had to go away elsewhere, and don't know what came true of the promise: I should not like to meet you that way, however.

My son is at Ch. Ch: [1] my owl is still on his perch: my book is out: my intention is to hear Joachim [2] play to-night: my friend is my friend, all the more because of Guido and the Lawyers— "What can I want beside?" as the psalm asks?

Ever yours,

R. B.

Sunday, Feb. 14 '69
Cumberland Place

I must write to you, my dear Mr. Browning, while my delight at the Pope's speech is fresh. Perhaps if I waited to finish Guido it might be too much diluted with remonstrance to do itself justice—and indeed, as it is, the mere subtraction sum performed in concluding the noble utterance and discovering the proportion it bears to the remainder makes me somewhat indignant. But inasmuch as nobody need read Guido's utterance unless he or she please, and no one could have read Innocent's unless you pleased, this is a some exacting and ungracious view of the matter. I feel as if there were more of that which seems to me your special message to us in the

---

[1] Christchurch College, Oxford.

[2] Joseph Joachim (1831-1907) has been described as the greatest master of the violin of his generation.

Pope's speech than in anything else you have written—it seems to me to leave my mind full of seeds. I say "It seems" and "I feel" in this tedious dilution, because after reading it only once I hardly know how far I have taken in *your* thoughts, and how far it is merely my own that are stirred and stimulated. I am sure that it brings us something of that ἔλεγχος οὐ βλεπομένων [1] that is not less the work of Poetry than the essence of faith. I felt for a while after reading it as if something in me were released, and could speak—now when I listen for it the words are all gone, yet I know that sense of everything falling into its place which it gave me—and I hardly feel with anything but Beethoven's music—means something large and permanent, which does not wax and wane with this capacity for utterance which it seems to awaken.

There is a sense of the great schism of life being healed in some chords of yours (not by any means in the old strain ever) that I have never felt equally in any one else. I can feel, as I listen to Innocent, that this poor little planet is a good inn for our souls to rest in, before they start on the long journey—no, not rest in, that is not the word, but I cannot find another. How

---

[1] Control of the things that are not seen.

truly you say we must speak lies, if we are to use language! If it were merely that one had to use a coarse pencil to delineate those subtle conceptions—but no, words are hoplessly impregnated with false association. But that sense of the wealth and glory of this life, and its insignificance—I can only hurry from one to the other, but you, in some rare flashes, shew me them together. This miserable incompleteness, this straining of the growing plant against the tiny pot, which in prosaic hours seems hopeless misfit and mistake, by *that* light turns into a promise. If we could believe we had an Eternity to work in, as we believe in June thro a snowy day of March! how easy then to bear—not perhaps the sharp ills of life, but all that makes it poor and fretful, all the misconception, thwarted plans, broken work, and that sense of incapacity and poverty within that is harder than all. It would be only then the changed attitude with which one wd put away a letter one had tried to read just before sunrise.

I pour out these incoherent ill-expressed feelings, because I feel sure in some way they are the echo to your thoughts, and yet I am aware they take so different a shape that I can fancy you may turn aside almost with irritation. I try to express what your thoughts arouse in *me*. I am sure it is a real effect of your words. "All harmony, all medicine is mine" (I am not quoting Shelley rightly.[1])—*that*, I feel, just touches the work of poetry. I can believe there is something besides I cannot understand, some more disinterested (so to speak) contemplation of things as they are, in which things foul and hideous have their place—yet this seems to me the ultimate test. I know you feel with me in this, though you admit so much that is apparently inconsistent with it. You do feel that your work is the deliverance of captives and the opening the eyes of the blind. If those wonderful flashes have ever shewn us a new Heaven and a new Earth, we do not quite go back to the old. Farewell—but I must finish what I have to say by and bye.

Yours ever,
F. J. W.

Sunday, Feb. 21, '69
Cumberland Place

DEAR FRIEND,

I feel, after finishing the Poem, as if I could not contemplate it without a sort of a squint.

---

[1] Shelley wrote "All prophecy, all medicine are mine" in the "Hymn of Apollo," stanza vi, line 4.

Or rather (for you, of all men, ought to have patience with an elaborate simile) it seems to me that a somewhat slight picture has been put into an elaborately carved frame which represents the same subject under a rather different point of view. I look at the Picture and I see a certain incident; I look at the frame and I see the same incident treated in a more ambitious style and with much greater fullness of detail. The result is that one hesitates which to look at.

For instance, Guido's last speech seems to me the epilogue to a long, dark, complicated elaborate story of intrigue and crime—an intricate web of treachery and cruelty, something of an Iago history. But Guido's actual part in the drama seems to one simply of stupid brutality. It is not merely that you enrich him with learning and fancy beyond what he would himself possess—I quite agree with you that tried by that test Shakespear would be undramatic. It is that you give him the kind of mind that fits on to a *different* set of actions. The mere brute, hacking Pompilia to pieces, seems to me to have nothing in common with the keen, subtle, intellectual pagan, sympathising with Virgil, reaching back into a remote past—giving evidence of so subtle and wily an intellect, as well as of such strong powers of hatred. I do not feel this double-ness so much in any other figure, yet I am not sure that there are not two Pompilias though *they* come much nearer together. In short, your subject seems to me too simple for you. This has not struck any one else, so I suppose I am wrong, but still I can't help saying what I think about it.

I do regret that so large a part of your canvas is spent in delineating what is merely hateful. But, of course, my first criticism somewhat cancels the force of the second. In all intellectual wickedness there is something not merely hateful, and so far as you have wandered from your historic theme, your aesthetic variation has gained. Still I *do* want not to have so much ugliness in the picture! Guido says he did not make himself—fit words to be put into the mouth of a liar! You know we make ourselves. I fancy neither you nor I are greatly delighted with this individuality of which so much is owing to the will of each, yet we do not accuse the great artist who sketched a soul we each copy so ill. My longing is to see *his* work copied—I do not say exclusively; it could hardly be made evident to us apart from our own scrawls—but at all events that this be the main thing, that what is presented to us be, on the whole, God's intention for man, not man's poor blurred distortion of that ideal. But I believe I am running into repetition of what I have said before, a course not desirable with the least patient of one's acquaintance!

Yes, I suppose your first summary of my criticism was true—I cannot sympathize in your choice of a subject. Surely I must be wrong here, you cannot have spent all these years on a mistake. I incline to think my nature is too undramatic, and I want all poetry to be direct utterance of some congenial feeling—this is narrow. Well, even this finds something to feed on in the poem in Innocent's speech and Pompilia's and a little of Caponsacchi's. I think it is very telling, the way you make the *real* Guido drop all insinuation about the two. I wish I knew how much historic warrant you have for your Innocent. I wish I could judge of your translation of Euripides. I feel a thirsty yearning towards those few first-hand thinkers of the world, but I can't get at them.

It seems so easy, comparatively, to go on a little further; but to make a beginning—one can hardly imagine the result which *now* would represent that effort in intellectual value. I wish I knew what you thought of the *"Gypsy."* It reminded me of you all through and yet I felt it thoroughly original.

I never go out anywhere except to my intimate friends when they are alone; even if I were in the habit I would avoid it, knowing your wish. I was very glad of all your scraps of news about yourself and your owl and your son and your concert. I am only not glad when I come to unreal words in any letter of yours. You know I am not inclined to sing an Anthem when I come to the end of your writings—under different circumstances I should not care, but as it is, I like my feeling to be spoken of just as it is. May I not see the next picture out of its frame? No, I daresay you wd rather not.

Farewell, my dear friend,

yr affectionate,

F. J. W.

Monday Afternoon

You well know I mean nothing by my words about the anthem, beyond what *you* mean when you hope, "I did not laugh too disrespectfully at your last letter"—why, the very spirit of truth is in these "lies," like an odour one has to imprison in an oil, or some such vehicle: *I* blush (for you) thinking what you please to imply in this allowance of "disrespectful laughter," if I be minded to profit thereby: am I really not to signify never so obliquely that I feel grateful for your listening so long to what . . . does not altogether please you? In another sense, I can believe, for more reasons than one, that you do and will patiently read what I write: more than that, I know my work is sincere, and not likely to abound in these days, and is at least worth examination,—even if you did not wish well to my working.

Yes, I got the letter you enquire about, but judged it inexpedient to clap my hands at the apparition of your praise like a moonrin, till I was out of the wood,—and, behold, I was soon ordained to knock my head against a tree! How could I expect you to like Guido? See, as long as you don't like, nay, hate—simply—I sympathise with you: tell me, "I hate the deed, and consideration of it"—nay, go on and add, "I object to anybody else considering such a deed,"— I understand, and, with a limitation, approve. I defend myself when you go beyond and urge, "And the deed could have no such motives nor circumstances." You write here—"Guido's part is simply one of stupid brutality"—to which neither does the cultivation, etc "*fit on*," nor with the keenness, subtlety, paganism, etc—nay, even if I understand you, even the treachery, intrigue, and Iago-qualities seem inappropriate to the product.

Why, I almost have you at an unfair disadvantage, in the fact that the whole story is *true!* How do *you* account for the "mere brutal hacking Pompilia to pieces" in a nobleman thirty years long the intimate of Cardinals: is this the case of a drunken operative that kicks his wife to death because she has no money for more gin? But I won't begin and tell my own story over yet another time,—I am too glad to get done with it. We differ apparently in our conception of what gross wickedness can be effected by cultivated minds,—I believe, the grossest—all the more, by way of reaction from the enforced habit of self denial which is the condition of men's receiving culture. Guido tried the over-refined way for four years, and in his rage at its unsuccess let the natural man break out.

It seems to me that Napoleon was capable, *mutatis mutandis*, of acting exactly as grossly and abominably as Guido: and that, on the large scale, he *did* act quite as falsely, as selfishly and cruelly. You must consider the matter for yourself: what I could find it in my heart to wonder that you don't see in the work is, that there *is*, or should be, "an utterance of congenial feeling" all the louder that it is not *direct*—I hoped it would be heard always by the side of, and *above*, all the disgusts and painfulnesses: is there anywhere other than an unintermitted protest (which would be worth nothing were it *loud*) against all the evil and in favour of all the good? Where does my *sympathy* seem diverse from yours so long as we watch the same drama? I quite allow you to refuse to watch. But I don't think that the general interests of the world allow certain other eyes to go and amuse themselves elsewhere. It seems somebody has just written a life of Lucrezia Borgia [1] on this principle of bidding the eye just see what it likes. He finds this and the other wickedness "impossible." *Who* commits the wickednesses that undeniably *are?* Last, I hold you are wrong even in your praise—that is, wrong in thinking that whatever you count white in Pompilia and Innocent could have come out as clearly without the black.

Here shall end my thought and concern about the thing, so far as regards you and your judg-

---

[1] *Lucrezia Borgia*, by W. Gilbert, was reviewed in the "Spectator," March 13, 1869, p. 326, the article following the review of *The Ring and the Book*, volumes III and IV.

ment about it. I will try and please you better
another time: yes, I have given four full years to
this "mistake," but what did I do with my four-
teen years in Italy? I must go on, busy myself
now, and rub my dry stick-like self into a blaze
in this cold evening of life. And whatever I
write I will always send you, and you will always
like to see it, will always speak your mind about
it, and will always be exactly in the relation that
you are now to

R. B.

(Feb. 22, 1869.)

Revd Prof. Maurice,[1]
Cambridge,
Mar. 5, '69

DEAR FRIEND,

It feels flat and dismal to have no more fuel
for my critical fire, and I like to write and tell
you so. However, I cannot say that my last stock
is quite exhausted yet, but perhaps the smoul-
dering flame finds more to feed on in your MS
than your printed sheets. I am amused to see with
what sudden impatience you turn from your production after your long absorption in it. I

---

[1] Frederick Denison Maurice (1805-1872), divine; inaugurated
the Working Men's College in Red Lion Square, London, in 1854;
Professor of moral philosophy at Cambridge, 1866.

hardly venture to reply to your last letter (at least, I should not venture unless the alternative of not reading my criticism was open to you) —that I allow you no advantage whatever from the fact of your material being history. "Tant pis pour les faits!" if they are not artistic. Fate has no conception of the fitness of things, you must not copy her bungling sketches, full as they are of false perspective and harsh coloring, but give us some relief from her coarse picture gallery by your truer representations.

Yes, truer; in this world I am sure often that what we see with our eyes is false. We have all done things quite out of keeping with our character—at least we seemed to do them, some whiff of strange circumstance coming at the critical moment against the arrow of will; in the world of poetry we must be sheltered from those gusts. However, as I read I mentally analyzed Guido into the historic brute and the fictitious Iago; probably I was wrong. You know how I shall thirst for his successor—or rather, you do not know at all.

I should have felt somewhat mortified to see how little you know, in the allusions which imply that ours has been a mutual relation—only that I think these are lies pure and simple—scentless oil, with no imprisoned odour. You are not really so arrogant, with all your arrogance, as to think that our shares were equal? My dear Friend, do not give me the utterly needless pain of having for a moment to think that you think it. Every act of mine during our short intercourse implied that this *could* not be—that I might merely consider myself. Whether I did wisely or unwisely for myself is not a matter I care to press on you or on any one. I think our common hunger for facts as they are is one thing that has drawn us together; do not let our intercourse be seen by any other light. Indeed, I am not unreasonable. I could bear to have the whole thing fade out of your mind, only not assume such a shape as you suggest (I do not say, design) when you say it was a loss to *you*. You know I turned to you almost as a survivor from some elder race. I stop to smile at my endeavour to turn that pyramid topsy-turvy. To have it copied as an hour-glass, or a figure of 8—!!!

There, there! I know it was all meant in kindness. The last words of your letter saddened me, yet I felt they must be true. The rare glow of your daylight must leave the evening chill, yet for myself I feel such an added preciousness to life with every gained height of thought, I wd

hope your wide horizon made up to you for almost everything—made up, that is, for all you
can lose. For is not the best what cannot be
lost? It is you who have most given me the
sense that the material world is a passing shadow
and that all which binds us each to each is
eternal.

I find the British Public is beginning to like
you well, for all minor poets seem to me to taste
of you. I don't like you in that form—but I
don't know that any one tastes good at second-
hand. Adieu.

I am yr ever affec.,

F. J. W.

Monday, March 8, '69

Honestly, I do not understand what you mean,
or, at least, *why* you mean what, on the whole,
I suppose you may. If I wanted to play at pick-
ing out causes of offence, I could charge you
with plenty of such by implication, offence, I
mean, in attributing real falseness to me—the
last thing in your thoughts, I well know.[1] There
was certainly as great a loss to me as to you—if I
treat you as I would be treated, and believe you

---

[1] Browning wrote "now."

—in the cessation of our intercourse. Now, why not? No playing and nonsense—in what respect was I left then with better resources than you? If you even meant such an enormous absurdity as that I saw more company, in one or another way, than you—first, I doubt the fact— I should not wonder if you had a face to face acquaintance with just as many men and women that count as such, as I had or have: then—resources of the other sort—you do not seriously talk to me in the strain of, "Ah, my gossip, you are older and more learned (in Guidoism) and a man!"—All I know is, that in some ambiguous way I am motioned to step up on to some pretty sort of pedestal whence I am to observe you somewhere below—which I decline doing.

I lost something peculiar in you, which I shall not see replaced,—is that stated soberly enough? I neither can—ever could, nor would, were I able,—replace anything I have once had: I think I *have* things thoroughly and effectually and, in a sense, sufficingly; it would be all the worse could I say to myself "These half-experiences may be expected   [1],—or, if the missing *halves* follow, *that* may do as well, and

---

[1] This word is illegible; it may be "recur" but there is no "to" before it.

be novel besides." But the acquiescence in absolute loss should remove all misconception or scruple as to what proves, when it subsequently presents itself,—gain,—new and unexpected. You now talk about having "done" something, "wisely or unwisely" for yourself: I shall not believe you ever "did" anything in the matter, but let *be*, let *do*—wisely, I have no doubt: I think you will not accuse me, after my four years' silence, with saying to the contrary,—for I am not given to "striving and crying."

Yes, the British Public like, and more than like me, this week, they let their admiration ray out on me, and at sundry congregations of men wherein I have figured these three or four days, I have seen, felt and, thru' white gloves, handled a true affectionateness not unmingled with awe— which all comes of the Queen's having desired to see me, and three other extraordinary persons, last Thursday: whereupon we took tea together and pretended to converse for an hour and twenty minutes; the other worthies, with the wives of such as were provided, being Carlyle, Grote and Lyell.[1] This eventful incident in my

---

[1] Thomas Carlyle (1795-1881); George Grote (1794-1871), banker and historian of Greece; Sir Charles Lyell (1797-1875), geologist. "The Court Circular," March 13, 1869, records that "Her Majesty on Thursday last had the pleasure of becoming personally

life—say, the dove descending out of heaven upon my head—seems to have opened peoples' minds at last: and provided the Queen don't send for the Siamese Twins,[1] the Beautiful Circassian Lady, and Miss Saurin,[2] as her next quartette-party, I am in a way to rise: you see, I am not disposed to contest that some "resources" *are!*

I think you are in the wrong about the proper treatment of facts—I don't say, as to *my* treatment of them. They want explaining, not altering. As to being "impatient with what has occupied me for years"—no: it is *done;* I occupy myself elsewhere, or else look elsewhither. Good-bye: I wish I could see you again: last Wednesday I sat at dinner close to an acquaintance of some thirty years,—he was very kind, and kept talking so long that I said "Come, we must go into the drawing-room." On Saturday he fell dead. He was wanting me to meet somebody at his house, whom I abstain from meeting, and he

---

acquainted with two of the most distinguished writers of the age—Mr. Carlyle and Mr. Browning. These eminent men—who, so far as intellect is concerned, stand head and shoulders above their contemporaries—were invited to meet the Queen at the residence of the Dean of Westminster."

[1] The Siamese Twins died in 1874 at the age of 60.

[2] Miss Saurin brought an action for wrongful and malicious conspiracy and libel against the Lady Superior of a convent. The trial lasted for nearly a month and the Lord Chief Justice's charge to the jury occupied nearly five columns of the "Times" of February 27, 1869. The plaintiff was awarded £500 damages.

urged that life was too short and uncertain to allow delay in the matter. I was obdurate notwithstanding.

Goodbye, again!

R. B.

Good Friday, 1869
Cumberland Place

I have been wishing to thank you for your last letter, dear friend, and perhaps if I could express the mixture of feelings it aroused in me, my response might be worthy of the attention of a student of Morbid Anatomy! But I greatly distrust my power of speaking the truth. I think this capacity—the suspected absence of which we resent as an insult—is in reality a gift as rare as genius. We seem forced to use "common forms" for the most individual and unique part of our experience. So, if I imply any falsity in you, it is no more than saying you are no better off than the rest of us, and on the whole I allow myself to hope that your last letter was that masterpiece of genius—a true utterance; true, that is, as far as you know. I say "I hope," for some of it was very welcome to me; that I "let be or let

· 184 ·

Robert Browning
(aged 57)
reading "The Ring and the Book" at Naworth Castle, September 19, 1869.
From a drawing by the Earl of Carlisle.
in the possession of Marchesa Edith Peruzzi dè Medici.

do wisely" was a very blessed assurance from you.

Dear friend, it was some refracted words of yours that made it possible to me to do as I did, (or what were represented as such). I was the seeker, you know. I think every step in our intercourse was initiated by me. My friendship with you was—is—the great blessing of my life, but it was impossible to me to carry on that outward indulgence of it after it had been implied to me, "He feels it a gêne." But why do I go back to this?—not certainly that I need occupy your thoughts with it. Not for a moment wd I cage the thoughts which I long to follow into the highest height and the lowest depth, in any minute personal speculations. If it were a question of blame to be divided between us (and I know it is not) no self-reproach could sting like any disappointment in you. But I cannot quite bear to hear you speak as if the intercourse which was preluded for me by years of the deepest sympathy, and which is remembered as the era of my life, had been a *mutual* gain—its interruption, a mutual loss. "In what respect were you left better off than I?" Subtract from that statement what is needed to make it true in your lips and the result will afford a very sufficient answer.

I smiled over your Teaparty. Yes, it is not *those* resources in which I envy you. You will tell me about what you take in hand next, won't you? I think I need not say whether every word of yours is precious to me. I wish I knew your sister.

Yrs ever,
F. J. W.

19 Warwick Crescent,
Upper Westbourne Terrace, W.
March 29, '69

I do not understand, from your letter, the whole importance of the statement in it that "it was some refracted words of mine, or what were represented to you as such, that made it possible," etc. And again, that other things were "impossible after it had been implied to you that 'they were felt as a gêne.' " You add "Why do I go back to this?" Ask rather—or I ask—what is this going forward to a quite new piece of information? I was certainly told that all happened through quite another kind of misapprehension,—a thing which, with my experience of peoples' power and will to apprehend rightly, I could easily imagine.

If you mean to say that, consequent to this, and as a facilitation to your acting upon it, came the report of these refracted words—well, I don't know whether, after all, there is any good of there having been reported this pure and simple untruth, any advantage, practically, to either of us: I considered, as I said then, and repeated in the words you quote, that in deferring to what I was bound to think the opinion of your family, no matter how mistaken in such a matter,[1] you "let be or let do wisely." I should have said something else could the fancy have crossed my mind that the "refracted words" entered into the question. I shall not put myself into the attitude of having ever uttered anything that could be so refracted by any stupidity conceivable, for the mere sake of pelting such a scarecrow simulation of what I am.

The opposite charge would have been not so absurd—that, out of the two or three occasions when I was induced to speak of you to your own friends, the mere honest expression of my sense of the value of your acquaintance might have been distorted by a foolish person, intending no malignity. I should not have seen the

---

[1] This word is not clear.

policy—had I stooped to try—in pretending to ignore a very patent thing, as if it were proper to undervalue a jewel lest one be supposed to meditate stealing it: I never went out of the way to praise it, but if somebody, some two or three times in all these years, came in mȳ way with a question,—I answered it. Now, don't suppose this new discovery gives me any particular undue pain: it is a little corroborative incident, quite consentaneous to my theory of the world and its ways.

It would be useless to argue out the advantages or disadvantages of two such different lives as yours and mine. I never implied, I hope, that I have not, nor always had, nearly all the conditions which make life happy.

It is also useless to dissertate upon uselessness. I enjoyed seeing you much,—there is a fact,—and acquiesced in giving up that enjoyment for any cause that seemed sufficient to you—there is another: and if you, of your very own self, could, however fantastically, assure me, "Oh, but it was all done to relieve *you* from a gêne!" —well, I shall say—"You know better!" I shall always give you as much as you care to take, of my labors or idlenesses of the literary kind. There is "a form in these things," as Lady Wilhelmina [1] says, a decent modesty which I am not unwilling to be troubled with—but, I dare think you do feel as kindly to me as you say: ask yourself whether you can disbelieve me when I repeat that my trust in that is one of my most precious possessions, and whether the old occasions when, every week at least, I could *inhale*—rather than be methodically apprized of the reality of such a possession, were "a gêne" to

 yours affectionately now, then and ever,

R. B.

I go, in ten days or a fortnight, to Paris for a month—letters are not sent to me when I travel.

Wednesday, Ap. 7, '69
Ravensbourne,
Beckenham

Yes, dear Friend, your reproof is no less just than unintentional—why should I "go forward to a piece of information" which must cause you annoyance and cannot greatly change the aspect of my conduct?—(for your hypothesis is substantially correct). It is excuse, not justification,

---

[1] Miss Carolina Wilhelmina Amelia Skeggs, in *The Vicar of Wakefield*, at the end of chapter XI.

that I so profoundly desired that you shd know —how multiform and complex were the influences which impelled me to the surrender of the most prized possession of my life. This is weak and superfluous. You know *me,* why should I care that you should accurately estimate an action which was only to a certain extent mine? Perhaps I am too unlike Lady Wilhelmina. Forgive me.

There was no malice or thoughtlessness in the "refraction" I spoke of. It was one of those subtle impressions which are potent in proportion to their vagueness; and urged upon me by one whose judgment I revered, I could not but yield. Do not import any image of bitterness into the transaction. Nothing was intimated to me but that that kind of apprehension which is not unnaturally created by such a friendship as ours, where one party has and the other has not— a centre for all the life of the heart—was shared by you. As there would be nothing insulting or unkind in such a suspicion from you, so neither was there anything of that nature in the feelings of those (who they were I know not) who infused this impression into your words. "With your experience of people's power" (do not add *will*) "to apprehend rightly" you must have witnessed many such illusions in your long experience of mankind. Perhaps I may say, without too much unwise revival, that your last letter greatly soothes the pain of these imagined expressions of yours; blame there was none to remove. Indeed this renewed intercourse with you, and the perception that you full realize my attitude towards you, takes from me a wonderfully large proportion of the pain of our separation.

What I feel about you does not occupy a large part of the surface of my mind—no feeling can which is not in any way linked with action. But nothing else casts its roots so deep, or comes so near the region where I am alone with God—and it is a satisfaction to me that you know this, for I think it lays a certain responsibility on every soul to have reflected that light for another, and so to be capable of obscuring it. One sentence of your letter I hardly understand, "I never implied, I hope, that I have not, nor always had, nearly all the conditions which make life happy." I shd have just inverted what you seem to say—that you *had* all and have them not. Yet I am very thankful for the assurance that *to have had* is enough for you. I shd like to squeeze out some impatience and contemptuousness from your letter and from yourself—just as

I might have wished to squeeze out Guido and the lawyers—but I suppose we must take you as you are.

You see how the British Public differs from me as to the value of what you have given us! If anything could convert you to my estimate I shd think it wd be this. But even this corroboration you will probably withstand. Please remember what you have written, "I shall always give you as much as you care to take of my labours" etc.—I wish you wd let me copy for you, you see how beautifully I can write. Perhaps you wd be afraid of any interpolating moral sentiments?—and it might be a danger. I hope your sojourn in Paris will be fragrant with blessed memories. Farewell.

Yr.
F. J. W.

Saturday, June 11, '70
Cumberland Place

I was going to begin in a sort of conventional way by saying "You will have forgotten me by this time"—but I feel so sure you will not, dear friend, in spite of every facility for oblivion, that I recall that preface only to disclaim it, and to make it the occasion of my saying that I do not need any word from you to tell me that it is erroneous.

I cannot help writing to try to pass on the impression made by Pompilia on a beautiful soul, among my friends. She said it made an impression on her that no work of art had ever approached, that she woke after reading it wondering what had made the world so different and feeling as if she must write to you to express her gratitude. She said it seemed to her the only thing that cd approach it in its effect was a beautiful sunset, that no music even was so pure and aspiring, that the character shone before her eyes like an upward flame.

You know I could not feel this, and you will know it was pleasant to me to meet with one who could. It seems hardly enough to say, but I like to say it, and there is no need to answer it. I felt a sort of revelation of blindness in that glow of admiration. I look for something from you that I can more fully enter into. You know you owe us an adequate translation of what your wife was to you. I am your always, dear friend,

J . . . .

(Signature torn away)

19 Warwick Crescent, W.
June 14, '70

DEAR FRIEND,

I have not forgotten you—depend upon that.
Thank you for sending me the opinion of your
"beautiful soul": do you know, I should be dis-
concerted and uneasy were it yours also: I don't
want you in that attitude. Nor, frankly, am I
a bit the more assured that my work is good because by some chance an unusually large number of my readers undoubtedly think so: but, as
frankly, I consider that your estimate of the
poem,—which is below my own estimate,—
ought to rise a little: of course, I speak only to
a point of fact and for precision in criticism—
you have in many other respects done me more
than justice out of the warmth and goodness of
your heart.

But why or how do I owe you—or whomso-
ever is included in "us"—any "adequate translation of what my wife was to me"?—except in
saying, as I devoutly do on other occasions than
sitting at meals, "For these and all other mercies
God be praised!" Let us show forth that praise
"not in our lips but in our lives."

Do you ever see the American newspapers?

Somebody has sent me an extract this morning containing the account of the glorification of poor Margaret Fuller,[1] wherein I was bothered to take part, but somehow understood the deprecatory gesture of my "genius." It is enough to make one devote oneself to Madame Schneider, heart, soul, body and members.

Come, let us go back to the quiet place, where we "do not forget each other." Goodbye, dear friend; it was very pleasant to hear your voice in the dark—though I see no face since years now.

R. B.

July 12, '70. Cumb. Pl.

There was a sentence in your letter of about a month ago that *my* genius made a move to answer, but time and space were adverse till now, when you have probably left London. "Why do I owe you any adequate translation of what my wife was to me?" I want to try to say what I meant in that sentence.

I cannot but look upon the gift of utterance as a debt, and indeed I know that you do too. "Not only with our lips" seems inapplicable

---

[1] Margaret Fuller (1810-1850); one of the leaders of the Transcendentalists and a pioneer in the women's rights movement; was associated with Emerson in founding the "Dial."

when the lips *are* the life. But what I specially demand is that no key shall be given in vain that all that has been learnt shall be—not of course taught, that wd be absurd, but represented. The struggle and misery of life is that we cannot believe humanity is Divine. This is the truth we need, in order to live, and we cannot reach it, because love and honor almost never run in one channel. And where this has been granted, I cannot bear that all the emphasis shd lie on the equally undeniable truth, Human beings are devilish. It seems to me ungrateful to come back from Eden to tell us that. I will not guard against such stupid misunderstandings as that I should seem to say, where is your Beatrice. But this one Sabbath should make all the week holy, and you who have been *satisfied* shd pass on that impression, when you have extracted all that was individual for your own holy of holies.

Now, dear friend, if this oracle seems to you to be uttering wonderful folly please keep that conviction to yourself and do not spend 1d in trying to convince a fellow creature of being a fool—it wd give me pain, which I know you wd not willingly do. Your enclosure made me much more nearly cry than laugh. Yrs ever affly,

F. J. W.

INDEX

ash